∞

Finding God's Will for You

Also available from
Sophia Institute Press
by St. Francis de Sales:

The Art of Loving God:
Simple Virtues for the Christian Life

Thy Will Be Done:
Letters to Persons in the World

St. Francis de Sales

Finding
God's Will
for You

SOPHIA INSTITUTE PRESS®
Manchester, New Hampshire

Finding God's Will for You is an excerpt of Books 8 and 9 from St. Francis de Sales's *Treatise on the Love of God,* translated by Rt. Rev. John K. Ryan, originally published in 1963 as an Image book by Doubleday and Company, Inc., Garden City, New York. This 1998 edition by Sophia Institute Press is published with the permission of the estate of John K. Ryan and contains minor editorial revisions and deletions throughout the text.

Cover design by Carolyn McKinney

Cover artwork: Phit 15 17 f.2v Psalter and New Testament: *David in prayer* / Biblioteca Medicea-Laurenziana, Florence, Italy / The Bridgeman Art Library International

Sophia Institute Press
Box 5284, Manchester, NH 03108
1-800-888-9344
www.SophiaInstitute.com
Sophia Institute Press® is a registered trademark of Sophia Institute.

Library of Congress Cataloging-in-Publication Data

Francis, de Sales, Saint, 1567-1622.
    [Traité de l'amour de Dieu. Book 8-9. English]
    Finding God's will for you / St. Francis de Sales.
        p. cm.
    Includes bibliographical references.
    ISBN 0-918477-83-2 (alk. paper)
    1. Spiritual life — Catholic Church. 2. God — Will. I. Title
BX2350.2.F69513 1998
241'.4 — dc21
                                        98-37143 CIP

∞

Contents

Editor's Note: The biblical references in the following pages are based on the Douay-Rheims edition of the Old and New Testaments. Where applicable, biblical quotations have been cross-referenced with the differing names and enumeration in the Revised Standard Version, using the following symbol: (RSV =).

∞

Finding God's Will for You

Chapter One

Recognize the goodness
of God's will

∞

Like good ground that has received seed and then in due season returns it a hundredfold,[1] a heart that has found complacence[2] in God cannot keep from wishing to render God another complacence in return. There is no one pleasing to us whom we do not desire to please. For a time cool wine refreshes those who drink it, but as soon as it has been warmed up by the stomach into which it has gone, it in turn warms up the stomach, and the more heat the stomach gives the wine, the more heat the wine returns. True love is never ungrateful, but strives to please those in whom it has found pleasure. From this fact arises that conformity among lovers that causes us to be like what we love. The most devout and most wise King Solomon became idolatrous and foolish when he began to love foolish, idolatrous women, and he had as many idols as his wives had.[3]

---

[1] Luke 8:8.

[2] Here St. Francis is speaking of an act of sacred love, which he discusses at length in Book 5 of his *Treatise on the Love of God*: "When we approve the good that we see in God and find joy in it, we make an act of complacence, for we find infinitely greater pleasure in the divine pleasure than in our own," *Treatise on the Love of God*, Bk. 5, ch. 1. — ED.

[3] 3 Kings 11:1-8 (RSV = 1 Kings 11:1-8).

Finding God's Will for You

∞

Strive to grow in God's likeness

This transformation is brought about imperceptibly by complacence. Once it has entered into our hearts, it produces another kind of complacence to give to Him from whom we received the first. It is said that in the Indies there is a little land animal that likes so much to be with fish in the sea that, by often swimming about with them, it finally becomes a fish itself and is changed completely from a land animal into a marine animal.[4] Thus, too, by often taking delight in God we become conformed to God, and our will is transformed into that of His divine majesty by the complacence it takes in Him. As St. John Chrysostom says, love either finds resemblance or produces it.[5]

The example of those we love has a mild, imperceptible empire and an insensible authority over us: we must either leave them or imitate them. When a man is attracted by the sweet odor of perfume and enters a perfumer's shop, he perfumes himself even while he receives the pleasure he takes in the smell of such odors. When he goes out, he gives others some of the pleasure he has received by spreading among them the scent of the perfume he has contracted. Along with the pleasure it takes in the thing loved, our heart attracts its qualities to itself. Delight opens up the heart, just as sorrow closes

---

[4] See L. de Almeyda, *Epistolae ex Japonica*, anno 1566.

[5] St. Jerome (c. 342-420); Biblical scholar, *Commentary on the prophet Micah*, Vol. 7. St. Francis mistakenly ascribed the passage to St. John Chrysostom (c. 347-407; Bishop of Constantinople). — TRANS.

it. Hence Holy Scripture often uses the word *enlarge* as in the expression "our heart is enlarged."[6]

When a man's heart has been opened by pleasure, the impressions of the qualities on which the pleasure depends easily enter into his mind. Along with them, other qualities in the same subject, even though displeasing to us, inevitably gain entry into us amid the throng of pleasures, just as the man without a wedding garment got into the banquet along with those who were properly dressed.[7] Thus Aristotle's disciples liked to speak with a lisp like his, and Plato's students walked with bent backs in imitation of him.[8]

To sum up, the pleasure we take in anything is a precursor that places in the lover's heart the qualities of the thing that pleases. Hence holy complacence transforms us into God, whom we love, and the greater the complacence, the more perfect the transformation. Thus, having great love, the saints are very quickly and perfectly transformed, since love transports and translates the manners and dispositions of one heart into another.

It is strange but true that when two lutes in unison — that is, with the same sound and pitch — are placed close together and someone plays one of them, although the other is untouched, it will not keep from sounding just like the one played on. The adaptation of one to the other is like natural love and

[6] Cf. 2 Cor. 6:11.

[7] Matt. 22:11.

[8] Aristotle (384-322 B.C.), Plato (427-347 B.C.), Greek philosophers. See Plutarch (c. 46-120; Greek biographer and historian), "How to Tell a Flatterer from a Friend," *Moralia*, Vol. 1, n. 53.

produces this correspondence. We dislike imitating those we hate even in their good qualities. The Lacedaemonians would not follow the good counsel of an evil man unless some good man stated it after him.[9]

On the contrary, we cannot help conforming ourselves to those we love. It is in this sense, I think, that the great apostle says that "the law is not made for the just."[10] In fact, the just man is not just unless he has holy love. If he has love, there is no need to urge him on with the rigor of the law, since love is a more cogent teacher and solicitor to persuade a heart possessing it to obey the will and intentions of its beloved. Love is a magistrate who exercises his authority without noise, without bailiffs or sergeants-at-arms, but merely by that mutual complacence whereby, just as we find pleasure in God, so also we reciprocally desire to please Him.

Love is the abridgment of all theology. In a most holy manner it turns into learning the ignorance of the Pauls, the Anthonys,[11] the Hilarions,[12] the Simeons,[13] and the Francises,[14] without books, without teachers, and without art. In virtue of

---

[9] See Plutarch, "Sayings of the Spartans," *Moralia*, Vol. 3.

[10] 1 Tim. 1:9.

[11] Probably St. Anthony of Egypt (c. 251-356), father of desert monasticism. — ED.

[12] St. Hilarion (c. 291-371), founder of the anchoritic life in Palestine.

[13] Probably St. Simeon Stylites (c. 390-459), the first of the pillar ascetics, those in the early Church who lived atop pillars. — ED.

[14] Possibly St. Francis of Assisi (c. 1181-1226), founder of the Franciscan Order, or St. Francis of Paola (1416-1507), founder of the order of friars known as Minims. — ED.

this love, the beloved bride can say with assurance: "My beloved is wholly mine, because of the complacence with which he pleases and feeds me, and I am wholly his because of the benevolence with which in turn I feed and please him. My heart feeds on the pleasure it takes in him, and his heart is fed because I take pleasure in him for his sake. Like a holy shepherd, he feeds me, his dear sheep amid the lilies[15] that are his perfections in which I take pleasure. As for me, his dear sheep, I feed him with the milk of my affections, by which I strive to please him." Whoever truly takes pleasure in God desires faithfully to please God and, in order to please Him, desires to conform to God.

ളు

Learn to submit to God's will

Complacence draws us into the mold of God's perfections according as we are capable of receiving them. We are like mirrors that receive the sun's image, not according to the perfection and vast extent of that great and wonderful luminary, but in proportion to the condition and size of its glass. It is thus that we are put into conformity with God.

Besides this complacence, the love of benevolence[16] gives us this holy conformity in another way. Love of complacence draws God into our hearts, but love of benevolence projects our hearts into God and consequently all our actions and affections, which it most lovingly dedicates and consecrates to Him. Good will desires for God all the honor, all the glory, and

---

[15] Cf. Cant. 2:16, 6:2 (RSV = Song of Sol. 2:16, 6:2).

[16] See *Treatise on the Love of God*, Bk. 5, ch. 6-12.

all the recognition that can be rendered Him as a kind of external good due to His goodness.

In accordance with the complacence we take in God, this desire is practiced in the following manner. After we have taken very great complacence in seeing that God is supremely good, then by the love of benevolence, we desire that all forms of love that can possibly be imagined should be employed so as to love this goodness in a proper way. We have taken delight in the supreme excellence of God's perfection, and as a result, we desire that He may be supremely loved, honored, and adored. We have rejoiced to consider that God is not only the first principle but also the last end, author, conserver, and Lord of all things. For this reason we desire that all things be subject to Him with supreme obedience. We see that God's will is supremely perfect, right, just, and equitable. After this consideration, we desire that His will may be the supreme rule and law of all things, and that it may be followed, served, and obeyed by all other wills.

But note, Theotimus,[17] that here I do not treat of obedience due to God insofar as He is our Lord and Master, our Father and benefactor. Obedience of this kind belongs to the virtue of justice and not to love. No, it is not that of which I speak at present. Even if there were no Hell to punish the rebellious and no Paradise to reward the good, and even if we had no kind of obligation or duty to God — all this must be said by way of imagining something impossible and hardly even imaginable — the love of benevolence would still impel

[17] Theotimus (literally, "one who honors God") is the one to whom St. Francis de Sales addresses his *Treatise on the Love of God*. — ED.

us to render complete obedience and submission to God by election and inclination; yes, even by a gentle, loving violence in consideration of the supreme goodness, justice, and rectitude of His divine will. Theotimus, we see how a young woman, by free choice proceeding from the love of benevolence, will subject herself to her husband to whom she previously owes no duty. We see, too, how a gentleman places himself at the service of a foreign prince, or even puts his will in the hands of the superior of some religious order that he wishes to join.

Thus, too, conformity of our heart with that of God is brought about when by holy benevolence we cast all our affections into the hands of His divine will so that they may be turned and directed as He chooses, and shaped and formed according to His good pleasure. In this point consists the most profound obedience of love, since it has no need to be roused up by threats or rewards or by any law or any commandment. It goes ahead of all such things when it submits itself to God because of that unique, most perfect goodness which is in Him. Because of this goodness, every will should be obedient, subject, and submissive to Him, and should be conformed and united forever, everywhere, and in all things to His divine intentions.

∝

Obey God's signified will

Sometimes we consider God's will in itself and see that it is all holy and all good. Hence it is easy for us to praise, love, and adore it and to sacrifice our will and the wills of all creatures to its obedience by making this divine prayer: "Your will be done on earth as it is in Heaven."[18] At other times we consider God's will in its particular effects, such as events that concern us and things that happen to us, and finally in the declaration and manifestation of His intentions. In reality His divine majesty has only one most unique and most simple will, although we call it by different names according to the various means by which we know it.

Moreover, in keeping with these various means, we are in different ways obligated to conform ourselves to His will. Christian doctrine clearly proposes to us the truths God wills us to believe, the goods He wills us to hope for, the punishments He wills us to fear, the things He wills us to love, the commandments He wills us to fulfill, and the counsels He desires us to follow. All this is called the signified will of God, because He has signified and made manifest His will and intention that all these things should be believed, hoped for, feared, loved, and practiced.

Because this signified will of God proceeds by way of desire and not by way of absolute will, we can either follow it by obedience or resist it by disobedience. In this regard God makes three acts of will: He wills that we should be able to resist; He desires that we should not resist; and yet He allows us to resist if we so will. That we *can* resist depends on our natural state and liberty; that we *do* resist depends on our own malice; and that we *do not* resist is according to the desire of divine goodness. Therefore, when we resist, God contributes nothing to our disobedience but leaves our will "in the hands of its own"[19]

---

[18] Matt. 6:10.
[19] Cf. Ecclus. 15:14.

free will and permits it to choose evil; when we obey, God contributes His assistance, His inspiration, and His grace.

Permission is an act of will that is of itself barren, sterile, and without fruit. It is as it were a passive action that does nothing but merely permits a thing to be done. On the contrary, desire is an active, fruitful, fertile action that excites, invites, and urges. Therefore, in His desire that we should follow His signified will, God solicits, exhorts, incites, inspires, assists, and rescues us, whereas in permitting us to resist, He simply lets us do what we wish to do according to our free choice, but contrary to His desire and intention.

Nevertheless this desire is a true desire. How can anyone more effectively express his desire that a friend should enjoy himself than to prepare a fine, good banquet, as did the king in the Gospel parable,[20] and then invite, urge, and almost compel him by pleas, exhortations, and pressing messages to come, sit down at the table, and eat? In fact if anyone would open a friend's mouth by force, cram food down his throat, and make him swallow it, he would not be affording him a courteous banquet but would be treating him like a beast — like a capon he wanted to fatten. A good deed of this kind must be offered by way of invitation, persuasion, and solicitation — not violently and forcibly thrust upon a man. Hence it is done by way of desire and not of absolute will.

It is the same with regard to God's signified will. By that will, God desires with true desire that we do what He makes known, and to this end He furnishes us with all things needed, and exhorts and urges us to use them. For a favor of this kind

[20] Matt. 22:2-10; Luke 14:16-23.

we can desire nothing more. Just as the rays of the sun do not cease to be true rays when shut out and thrust back by some obstacle, so God's signified will does not cease to be God's true will when we resist it, even though it does not produce as many effects as it would if we had cooperated with it.

Therefore the conformity of our heart with God's signified will consists in the fact that we will all that God's goodness signifies to us as His intention, so that we believe according to His teaching, hope according to His promises, fear according to His warnings, and love and live according to His ordinances and admonitions.

All those protestations we make so often in the Church's holy ceremonies tend to this end. For this reason we remain standing while the Gospel is read to show that we are ready to obey the holy signification of God's will contained in the Gospel. For this reason we kiss the book at the place where the Gospel is, to show that we adore the holy word that declares God's will. For this reason, in ancient days, many men and women saints bore upon their breasts the Gospel written out as a talisman of love, as is told of St. Cecilia.[21] In fact, St. Matthew's Gospel was found on St. Barnabas'[22] heart after his death, written out in the saint's own hand.

Finally, because of this, in the early councils they set up a throne in the midst of all the assembled bishops and placed on it the book of the holy Gospels to represent the person of the Savior, king, teacher, director, spirit, and unique heart both of

[21] St. Cecilia, second- or third-century martyr and patroness of Church music.

[22] St. Barnabas, "son of encouragement" (Acts 4:36), early Christian disciple martyred in the year 61.

the councils and of the entire Church. So greatly did they honor the signification of God's will as expressed in that divine book! Indeed, the great mirror of the pastoral order, St. Charles Borromeo,[23] Archbishop of Milan, never studied Holy Scripture except on his knees and with uncovered head to testify to the respect with which we must hear and read God's signified will.

∞

Resolve to cooperate with God's will to save you

God has signified to us in so many ways and by so many means that He wills all of us to be saved, that no one can be ignorant of this fact. For this purpose He made us "in His own image and likeness"[24] by creation, and by the Incarnation, He has made Himself in our image and likeness, after which He suffered death in order to ransom and save all mankind. He did this with so great a love that, as St. Dionysius, the apostle of France, relates, He once said to Carpus, a holy man, that He was "ready to repeat His passion in order to save man," and that this would be pleasing to Him if it could be done without any man falling into sin.[25]

Although all men are not saved, this will that all should be saved still remains God's true will, for He acts in us according to the condition of His own nature and of ours. His goodness moves Him to communicate liberally to us the help of His grace

[23] St. Charles Borromeo (1538-1584), one of the leaders of the Counter-Reformation.

[24] Cf. Gen. 1:26-27.

[25] St. Dionysius the Areopagite (early Christian converted by St. Paul), *Letter to Demophilus*, Letter 8, sect. 6.

so that we may come to the joy of His glory, but our nature requires that His liberality should leave us at liberty to use it for our salvation or to neglect it to our damnation.

"One thing I have asked of the Lord; it is this that I shall seek after forever: that I may see the delight of the Lord and visit His temple,"[26] says the psalmist. What is the delight of supreme goodness except to pour forth and communicate His perfections? Truly His "delights are to be with the children of men,"[27] and to turn His graces upon them. For free agents, nothing is so agreeable and delightful as to do their own will. Our "sanctification is the will of God,"[28] and our salvation is His good pleasure.

There is no difference between good pleasure and good delight, and consequently none between divine good delight and the divine good will. Hence God's will to do good to men is called good because it is amiable, kind, favorable, and agreeable. And, as the Greeks, following St. Paul, have said, it is true philanthropy; that is, benevolence, or a will filled with love for men.[29]

That whole heavenly temple that is the Church, both triumphant and militant,[30] resounds on every side with canticles of God's sweet love for us. The most sacred body of our Savior, like a most holy temple of His divinity, is decorated on every

---

[26] Ps. 26:4 (RSV = Ps. 27:4).

[27] Cf. Prov. 8:31.

[28] Cf. 1 Thess. 4:3.

[29] Titus 3:4; Acts 28:1.

[30] The Church Triumphant refers to the body of Christians in Heaven, and the Church Militant, the body of Christians on earth.

side with the marks and insignia of this benevolence. Hence when we visit the divine temple, we behold that loving delight which His heart takes in doing us favors. Therefore a hundred times during the day we should turn our gaze upon God's loving will, make our will melt into it, and devoutly cry out, "O Good of infinite sweetness, how amiable is Your will and how desirable are Your favors! You have created us for eternal life, and Your maternal bosom abounds in the milk of mercy, whether to pardon penitents or to make perfect the just. Ah, why do we not fasten our wills to Yours, to draw from it Your eternal blessings!"

Theotimus, we must will our own salvation just as God wills it. God wills it by way of desire, and following His desire, we also must incessantly desire it. Not only does He will it, but in effect He gives us all the means we need to attain it. Therefore, as a result of our desires to be saved, we must not only will but actually accept all the graces He has prepared for us and offers to us. It is enough to say, "I desire to be saved," but it is not enough to say, "I desire to embrace the means suitable to arrive at salvation." With absolute resolution we must will and embrace the graces God presents to us, for our will must correspond to God's will. Insofar as His will gives us the means of salvation, we must receive them, just as we must desire salvation as God desires it for us and because His will desires it.

It sometimes happens that the means of attaining salvation, considered en masse or in general, are agreeable to our hearts, while they terrify us when considered in detail and in particular. We have seen poor St. Peter ready to accept all kinds of hardship in general — even death itself — in order to follow his

Master.[31] Yet when it comes to actual fact and performance, St. Peter turns pale, trembles, and at the word of a simple serving maid denies his Master.[32] We think that we can drink our Savior's chalice with Him,[33] but when it is actually presented to us, we run away; we give up everything.

Things proposed in detail make stronger impressions and more sensibly strike the imagination. For this reason, we have advised in the *Introduction*[34] that after general affections, we make particular resolutions in holy prayer. David accepted particular afflictions as an advancement toward perfection when he sang in this way: "O Lord, it is good for me that You have humbled me, that I might learn Your justification."[35] So also the apostles were joyful in their tribulations because they had been counted worthy to suffer ignominy for their Savior's name.[36]

Obey God's commandments out of love for Him

God's desire to make us observe His commandments is supremely great, as all Scripture witnesses. How could He express it better than by the great rewards He sets before keepers of His law, and the awesome punishments with which He threatens its violators? For this reason David cries out, "O

---

[31] Luke 22:33.
[32] Luke 22:56-57.
[33] Matt. 20:22; Mark 10:38-39.
[34] See *Introduction to the Devout Life*, Part 2, ch. 6.
[35] Cf. Ps. 118:71 (RSV = Ps. 119:71).
[36] Acts 5:41.

Lord, You have commanded that Your commandments be kept most diligently."[37]

When the love of complacence sees this divine desire, it wishes to please God by observing it. As a consequence, the love of benevolence, which wishes to submit all things to God, submits our desires and our wills to that which God has signified to us. From this there issues not only observance but also love of the commandments. David extols this in an extraordinary way in Psalm 118, which he seems to have composed only for this purpose:

> With heart aflame I love Your will and way,
> On it alone I think and speak all day!
> Better than glittering topaz and pure gold
> I cherish, Lord, Your laws laid down of old!
> So sweet to me is what Your tongue declared,
> Bitter all honey grows with it compared![38]

To arouse in ourselves such holy, salutary love of the commandments, we must contemplate their wondrous beauty. Just as certain deeds are evil because they are forbidden, while others are forbidden because they are evil, so also certain deeds are good because they are commanded, while others are commanded because they are good and very useful. Therefore, all of them are very good and worthy of love, because the commandment gives goodness to those which otherwise would lack it and an increase of goodness to those others which would still be good even if not commanded.

[37] Cf. Ps. 118:4 (RSV = Ps. 119:4).
[38] Cf. Ps. 118:97, 127, 103 (RSV = Ps. 119:97, 127, 103).

We do not receive a good graciously when it is presented to us by an enemy's hand. On the contrary, a present is always acceptable when a friend makes it. The sweetest commandments become bitter if a cruel, tyrannical heart imposes them, and they become most pleasing when ordained by love. Jacob's service seemed a royal thing to him because it proceeded from love.[39] Ah, how sweet and desirable is the yoke of heavenly law placed on us by so loving a King!

Many men keep the commandments in the way sick men take medicine: more from fear of dying in damnation than for joy of living according to our Savior's will. Just as some persons dislike taking medicine, no matter how pleasant it is, simply because it is called medicine, so there are some souls who hold in horror things commanded simply because they are commanded. There was a certain man, it is said, who had lived contentedly in the great city of Paris for eighty years without ever leaving it. However, as soon as he was enjoined by the king to remain there for the rest of his days, he left the city to see the country which he had never wanted to see during his previous life.

On the contrary, a loving heart loves the commandments. The more difficult they are, the sweeter and more agreeable it finds them, since this more perfectly pleases the Beloved and gives Him greater honor. It pours forth and sings hymns of joy when God teaches it His commandments and justifications.[40] The pilgrim who goes on his way joyously singing adds the labor of singing to that of walking, and yet by this increase of

---

[39] Cf. Gen. 29:20.
[40] Cf. Ps. 118:171 (RSV = Ps. 119:171).

labor, he actually lessens his weariness and lightens the hardship of the journey.

In like manner the devout lover finds such sweetness in the commandments that nothing in this mortal life comforts and refreshes him as much as the gracious burden of God's precepts. Because of this, the holy psalmist cries out, "O Lord, Your justifications" — that is, commandments, — "are sweet songs to me in this place of my pilgrimage."[41]

It is said that mules and horses laden with figs quickly fall beneath their burden and lose all their strength. Sweeter than figs is the law of the Lord, but a brutish man, who has become like "the horse and the mule, who have no understanding,"[42] loses courage and cannot find the strength to bear this dear burden. On the contrary, just as a spray of *agnus castus* keeps a traveler who bears it about with him from becoming weary,[43] so also the cross, the mortification, the yoke, and the law of our Savior, who is the true "chaste lamb,"[44] are a burden that takes away weariness and refreshes and restores hearts that love His divine majesty. "There is no toil in what we love, or if there is any, it is a beloved toil."[45] Toil mingled with holy love is bittersweet; a thing more pleasant to taste than what is entirely sweet.

---

[41] Cf. Ps. 118:54 (RSV = Ps. 119:54).

[42] Ps. 31:9 (RSV = Ps. 32:9).

[43] *Agnus castus* is the name of an ornamental shrub that bears a blue or white flower. See Pliny the Elder, *Natural History*, Bk. 14, ch. 38.

[44] Cf. 1 Pet. 1:19.

[45] St. Augustine (354-430; Bishop of Hippo), *De bono viduitatis*, ch. 21.

Finding God's Will for You

Thus does divine love conform us to God's will and make us carefully observe His commandments as the absolute desire of His divine majesty, which we wish to please. Therefore, this complacence with its sweet and amiable violence goes in advance of that necessity to obey, which the law imposes upon us, and converts such necessity into the virtue of love, and all difficulty into delight.

∝

Serve God in the circumstances in which He places you

A commandment bears witness to a most complete and urgent will in the one who orders it, but a counsel represents only a will of desire. A commandment renders its transgressors culpable, but a counsel only renders those who do not follow it less worthy of praise. Those who violate commandments deserve damnation; those who neglect counsels merit only to be less glorified.

There is a difference between commanding and recommending: when we command, we use our authority to impose obligation; when we recommend, we make use of friendship to persuade and exhort. A commandment imposes strict obligation; counsel and recommendation arouse us to something of greater utility. Obedience corresponds to command; belief, to counsels. We follow counsels in order to please, but commandments lest we displease.

For this reason, love of complacence, which obliges us to please our Beloved, consequently carries us on to follow His counsels, while love of benevolence, which desires all wills and affections to be subject to the Beloved, causes us to will not only what He ordains but also what He counsels and exhorts us to do. It is like the love and respect a good child has for a good father, for such love makes him resolve to live not only according to the commandments his father imposes, but also according to the desires and preferences he manifests.

A counsel is given to the man we counsel so that he may become perfect. "If you will be perfect," says the Savior, "go, sell what you have, and give to the poor, and come, follow me."[46] A loving heart does not accept a counsel because of some practical advantage, but to conform to the counselor's desire and to render him the homage due his will. Therefore, it does not accept counsels except in such manner as God desires. Moreover, God does not desire that each and every man should observe all the counsels, but only such counsels as are suitable according to differences in persons, times, occasions, and abilities as charity requires. It is charity, as queen of all virtues, all commandments, and all counsels — in short, of all Christian laws and works — that gives all of them their rank, order, season, and value.

When your father or mother actually needs your help in order to live, it is not the time to practice the counsel of retirement to a monastery. Charity requires that you actually put into execution its command to honor, serve, aid, and relieve your father or mother.[47] You are a prince, and by your line, subjects of your crown are to be kept in peace and safe from tyranny, sedition, and civil war. The need for so great a good obligates you to beget lawful successors in holy marriage. To do so is not to lose chastity — or at least it is to lose it chastely —

[46] Cf. Matt. 19:21; Luke 18:22.
[47] Exod. 20:12.

but to sacrifice it for the public good and for the sake of charity.

Is your health weak, uncertain, and in need of great care? If so, do not voluntarily undertake actual poverty, since charity forbids it to you. Charity not only does not permit fathers of families to sell all things so as to give to the poor; it also commands them to accumulate honestly what is needed for the education and support of wife, children, and servants. So also it commands kings and princes to possess treasures, which, since they have been gained by praiseworthy economy and not by tyrannical measures, serve as salutary defenses against visible enemies. Does not St. Paul counsel the married that after giving time to prayer, they should return to the well-ordered course of married love?[48]

All the counsels are given for the perfection of Christian people, but not for that of each particular Christian. There are circumstances that make them sometimes impossible, sometimes unprofitable, sometimes dangerous, and sometimes harmful to certain men. This is one of the reasons why our Lord says about one of them what He wishes to be understood of all: "Let him who can accept it accept it."[49] According to St. Jerome, it is as though he said that a man who can win and carry off the honor of chastity as a prize of renown should take it, for it is set before those who shall run valiantly. Hence, not all men are able — that is, it is not expedient for all men, always to observe all the counsels. Since they are granted for the sake of charity, charity is the rule and measure for their fulfillment.

[48] 1 Cor. 7:5.

[49] Cf. Matt. 19:12: a reference to the vow of virginity. — TRANS.

Recognize the goodness of God's will

Therefore, when charity so orders, monks and religious are taken out of their cloisters to be made cardinals, prelates, and parish priests; sometimes they are even led into marriage for the peace of a kingdom, as I have already stated. If charity causes men who had bound themselves by solemn vows to leave their cloisters, then for greater reason and for less cause, by authority of this same charity, we can counsel many men to remain at home, to keep up their property, to marry, or even to take up arms and go to war, which is so dangerous a profession.

When charity leads some men to poverty and draws others away from it, when it directs some to marriage and others to continence, when it encloses one person in the cloister and causes another to leave it, it does not need to render reasons to anyone. Charity has the fullness of power under Christian law according to what is written, "Charity can do all things."[50] It has the perfection of prudence, according to the words, "Charity does nothing in vain."[51] If anyone would challenge this and ask why charity does this, charity will answer boldly, "Because the Lord has need of it."[52] All things are made for charity, and charity is made for God. All things must serve charity, but charity serves none, not even its Beloved. It is not His servant, but His spouse, and charity does not offer Him service but gives Him love. For this reason we must take from charity the order in which we exercise the counsels. To some, charity will appoint chastity but not poverty; to others, obedience but not chastity; to others, fasting but not almsgiving; to others, solitude

[50] Cf. 1 Cor. 13:7.
[51] Cf. 1 Cor. 13:8.
[52] Cf. Matt. 21:3.

25

and not care of souls; to others, association with men and not solitude.

To sum up, charity is sacred water by which the garden of the Church is made fertile. Although charity itself is colorless, the flowers that it makes spring up have each of them a different color. Charity makes martyrs redder than the rose and virgins whiter than the lily. To some, it gives the fine violet of mortification, and to others, the yellow of marriage cares. In various ways, it employs the counsels for the perfection of souls that are happy to live under its sway.

Chapter Two

*Keep a steady course in
the pursuit of holiness*

꩜

How worthy of love is this divine will, Theotimus! How worthy of love and desire! O law that is all of love and all for love! By the word *peace*, the Hebrews understood the sum total and perfection of all good things; that is, felicity. The psalmist cries out, "Those who love God's law have great peace, and for them there is no stumbling block,"[53] as if to say, "O Lord, what delights there are in the love of Your sacred commandments! All delightful sweetness seizes the heart seized by love of Your law." In fact, that great king whose heart was made according to God's heart relished so keenly the perfect excellence of divine ordinances that he seems like a lover captivated by the beauty of that law as though it were the chaste spouse and queen of his heart.[54] It is thus that it appears from the continual praises he gives to it.

꩜

Love all the counsels of our Lord
When the heavenly bride wishes to express how infinitely sweet are her divine Spouse's perfumes, she says to Him, "Your

---

[53] Cf. Ps. 118:165 (RSV = Ps. 119:165).

[54] Cf. 1 Kings 13:14 (RSV = 1 Sam. 13:14); Acts 13:22. St. Francis is referring to David. — ED.

name is a spreading ointment,"[55] as if to say: "You are so well perfumed that You seem to be all perfume, and that it is proper to call You ointment and perfume itself rather than say You are anointed and perfumed." So the soul that loves God is so transformed into the divine will that it merits to be described as the will of God rather than as obedient and subject to His will.

Hence God says through Isaiah that He will call the Christian Church "by a new name, which the mouth of the Lord shall name,"[56] stamp, and engrave on the hearts of His faithful. Then He explains this name and says that it shall be "My will in her,"[57] as if to say that among non-Christians, each man has his will deep in his own heart, while among the Savior's true children, everyone shall forsake his own will, and there shall be but one master, dominant, universal will that shall animate, govern, and direct all souls, all hearts, and all wills. Among Christians the name of honor shall be none other than "God's will in them," the will that shall rule over all wills and transform them all into itself, so that the will of Christians and the will of our Lord may be but one single will.

This was perfectly expressed in the primitive Church, when, as the glorious St. Luke says, "In the multitude of the believers there was but one heart and one soul."[58] He does not mean to speak of the heart that keeps our body alive, or the soul that animates the heart with human life. He speaks of the

[55] Cf. Cant. 1:2 (RSV = Song of Sol. 1:2).
[56] Isa. 62:2.
[57] Cf. Isa. 62:4.
[58] Cf. Acts 4:32.

heart that gives heavenly life to our souls and of the soul that animates our heart with supernatural life. These are the most unique heart and the most unique soul of true Christians, and they are simply the will of God.

"Life is in the will of God,"[59] says the psalmist, not only because our temporal life depends on the divine will, but also because our spiritual life consists in its fulfillment, by which God lives and reigns in us and makes us live and subsist in Him. On the contrary, "the wicked man from of old" — that is, always — "has broken the yoke" of God's law and has said, "I will not serve."[60] For this reason God says that from his mother's womb He has called him a transgressor and rebel.[61] When He speaks to the King of Tyre, He reproaches him for having "set his heart as if it were the heart of God,"[62] for the spirit of revolt would have its heart as its own master, and its will supreme like the will of God. Such a heart does not want God's will to reign over its will, but wishes to be absolute and without any dependence whatsoever.

> Eternal Lord, permit not this, but ensure that
> forever "not my will but Yours be done." Ah,
> we are in this world not to do our own will but
> that of Your goodness, which has placed us here.
> It was written of You, O Savior of my soul, that
> You did the will of Your eternal Father. By the
> first human act of will of Your soul at the instant

[59] Cf. Ps. 29:6 (RSV = Ps. 30:5).
[60] Jer. 2:20.
[61] Cf. Isa. 48:8.
[62] Cf. Ezek. 28:2.

31

of Your conception, You lovingly embraced that
law of the divine will and placed it within Your
heart, eternally to reign and have dominion there.

Ah, who will give my soul the grace to have no will but the
will of God!

When our will is very close to God's will, we are not content to do only the divine will which is signified to us by the
commandments; we also place ourselves under obedience to
the counsels, which are given to us only for more perfect observance of the commandments, to which they are also re-
lated, as St. Thomas so excellently states.[63] How strictly does a
man observe the prohibition of illicit pleasures if he has renounced even the most just and licit delights! How far is he
from coveting another's goods who rejects all wealth, even
such as he might have kept in a holy manner! How far from
preferring his own will above that of God is he who, to do
God's will, submits himself to that of another man!

One day "David was in his camp, and there was a garrison
of the Philistines in Bethlehem. And David longed and said,
'Oh, that some man would give me a drink of water out of the
cistern that is in Bethlehem by the gate.' "[64] He had no sooner
said these words than three valiant knights went out with
hands and heads lowered, passed through the enemy's camp,
went to the cistern in Bethlehem, drew out the water, and
brought it to David. When he saw the danger that these three

---

[63] St. Thomas Aquinas (1225-1274; Dominican philosopher and
theologian), *Summa Theologica*, II-II, Q. 189, art. 1.

[64] 2 Kings 23:15 (RSV = 2 Sam. 23:15).

chivalrous men had run to gratify his appetite, "he would not drink" that water obtained at peril of their blood and life, but "poured it out in sacrifice" to the eternal God.[65]

Ah, see, I beg of you, Theotimus, how great is the ardor of those knights to serve and satisfy their master! They fly, they break through their enemies' ranks, they incur a thousand dangers of destruction to satisfy a single simple desire that their king expresses to them.

When our Savior was in this world, He declared His will in many things by way of commandment, but in many others He only signified it by way of desire. He gave high praise to chastity, poverty, obedience, and perfect resignation, denial of one's own will, widowhood, fasting, and continual prayer. What He says of chastity — namely, that he who could carry off the prize should take it[66] — He says in sufficient measure of all other counsels. Because of this desire, the most valiant Christians have entered the race. Overcoming all repugnance, concupiscence, and hardship, they have attained to holy perfection by binding themselves to strict observance of their King's desires. By such means they have obtained the crown of glory.

Truly, as the divine psalmist testifies, God hears not only the prayers of His faithful, but even their very desires and the very preparation they make in their hearts for prayer,[67] so favorable and so propitious is He to do the will of those who love him.[68] Why, then, shall we not in turn be so zealous to follow

---

[65] 2 Kings 23:16-17 (RSV= 2 Sam. 23:16-17).

[66] Cf. Matt. 19:12.

[67] Ps. 9b:17 (RSV = Ps. 10:17).

[68] Cf. Ps. 144:19 (RSV = Ps. 145:19).

our Lord's sacred will that we not only do what He commands but also what He tells us to be His liking and wish? Generous souls need no stronger motive for embracing a project than the knowledge that their beloved desires it. "My soul," says one of them, "melted as soon as my beloved spoke."[69]

∞

Never cease to aim for perfection

The words in which our Lord exhorts us to aspire and strive toward perfection are so strong and urgent that we cannot falsify our obligations to undertake that design. "Be holy because I am holy,"[70] He says. "He that is holy, let him be sanctified still more, and he that is just, let him be still more justified."[71] "Be perfect, as your heavenly Father is perfect."[72] For this reason when the great St. Bernard[73] wrote to the abbot of Aux, St. Guerin,[74] whose life and miracles have left so sweet an odor in this diocese, he said: "The just man never says it is enough; he always 'hungers and thirsts for justice.' "[75]

In temporal matters, Theotimus, it is true that nothing is sufficient for one who is not satisfied with what is enough. What can suffice a heart to whom sufficiency is insufficient?

---

[69] Cf. Cant. 5:6 (RSV = Song of Sol. 5:6).

[70] Lev. 11:44; 1 Pet. 1:16.

[71] Cf. Rev. 22:11.

[72] Matt. 5:48.

[73] St. Bernard (1090-1153; Abbot of Clairvaux), *Epistole 254, Ad Abbatem Guarimum Alpensem*, no. 2.

[74] St. Guerin, also known as St. Guarinus (died 1150), Bishop of Sion.

[75] Cf. Matt. 5:6.

But in spiritual goods, the man who is content to have what suffices *does not have* what suffices. Sufficiency is not sufficient, because true sufficiency in the things of God consists partly in desire for affluence. At the beginning of the world, God commanded the earth to bring forth "the green herb, bearing its seed, and every fruit tree yielding fruit, each after its kind, which also has its seed in itself."[76] We know from experience that plants and fruit trees have not reached full growth and maturity until they have brought forth seeds and pods that serve to raise up other trees and plants of the same kind.

Our virtues never come to full stature and maturity until they beget in us desires for progress, which, like spiritual seeds, serve for the production of new degrees of virtue. I think that that earth which is our heart has been commanded to bring forth plants of virtue bearing the fruits of holy works, "each one after its kind," and having as seeds desires and plans of ever multiplying and advancing in perfection. A virtue that does not produce the seed or kernel of such desires has not yet come to its full growth and maturity.

To the drone St. Bernard says, "So, then, you do not want to advance in perfection?"

"No."

"Nor yet grow worse?"

"No, indeed."

"What, then, you would be neither better nor worse? Alas, my poor fellow, you want to be what cannot be. In this world, nothing is either lasting or stable, but even more especially it

---

[76] Cf. Gen. 1:11.

is said of man that 'he never remains in the same state.' "[77] It is necessary, then, for a man either to advance or go backward.

Now, no more than St. Bernard do I say that it is a sin not to practice the counsels. Certainly not, Theotimus. The precise difference between a commandment and a counsel is that a commandment obligates us under pain of sin, while a counsel merely invites us without pain of sin. Nevertheless, I emphatically say that to despise aiming at Christian perfection is a great sin, and that it is a still greater sin to despise the invitation by which our Lord calls us to it. Moreover, it is intolerable impiety to despise the counsels and the means for the attainment of Christian perfection that our Lord shows to us. It is heresy to say that our Savior has not given us good counsel. It is blasphemous to say to God, "Depart from us; we do not wish to learn Your ways."[78] It is horrible irreverence to Him who with so much love and sweetness invites us to perfection, to say, "I do not want to be holy, or perfect, or to have a greater share in Your friendship, or to follow the counsels You give me to advance in it."

It is true that a man may refrain from following the counsels without sin because of an affection of some other kind that he has. For example, a man can rightly refrain from selling what he possesses and giving it to the poor because he lacks courage to make so complete a renunciation. It is also licit for a man to marry, because he loves a certain woman, or because he lacks sufficient strength of mind to undertake the war that

[77] St. Bernard, *Epistole 254, Ad Abbatem Guarinum Alpensem*, no. 2; Job 14:2.
[78] Cf. Job 21:14.

must be waged against the flesh. But to proclaim that one does not wish to follow the counsels — not any of them — cannot be done without contempt of Him who gives them.

Not to follow the counsel of virginity in order to marry is not to do wrong; but to marry because you regard marriage as a higher state than celibacy, as heretics do, is great contempt either of the counselor or of the counsel. To drink wine against the doctor's advice when one is overcome by thirst or by desire to drink is not precisely to despise the doctor or his advice. But to say, "I will not follow the doctor's advice" must necessarily proceed from a bad opinion one has of him.

But with regard to God, to reject and despise His counsel can only come from the idea that He has not given us good counsel. Such a thing can be thought only in a spirit of blasphemy, as though God were either not wise enough to know or not good enough to wish to give good advice. It is the same with regard to the counsels of the Church, for with the continued assistance of the Holy Spirit, who teaches and guides it "in all truth,"[79] the Church can never give bad advice.

∞

Practice the counsels that are
suited to your state of life

Although all the counsels cannot and should not be practiced by each individual Christian, everyone is bound to love them all, since they are all most good. If you have a sick headache and the odor of musk annoys you, will you for that reason refuse to admit that such scent is good and agreeable? If a

[79] John 16:13.

golden robe is not becoming to you, will you say that it is of no value? If a ring does not fit your finger, will you therefore throw it away as trash?

Theotimus, you should praise and dearly love all the counsels God has given to men. Blessed forever be the "Wonderful Counselor"[80] together with all the words of advice He gives and all the exhortations He makes to men! "Ointments and perfumes rejoice the heart, and the good counsels of a friend are sweet to the soul,"[81] says Solomon. Of what friend and of what counsels do we speak? We speak of the friend of friends, and His counsels are more pleasing than honey. That friend is the Savior; His counsels are for our salvation.

Theotimus, let us rejoice when we see others undertake to follow counsels that we cannot or must not observe. Let us pray for them, bless them, favor them, and assist them. Charity places an obligation on us to love not only what is good for ourselves, but also what is good for our neighbor.

We give sufficient testimony to our love for all the counsels when we devoutly observe those suitable to ourselves. A man who believes one article of Faith because God has revealed it by His word and announced and declared it by His Church cannot disbelieve the others. A man who observes one commandment out of true love of God is most ready to observe the others when occasion presents itself. In like manner, a man who loves and prizes one evangelical counsel because God has given it cannot help prizing all the others in turn, since they, too, are from God. We can easily practice some of them, but

---

[80] Isa. 9:6.
[81] Prov. 27:9.

not all of them together. God has given many counsels so that each of us can observe some of them. No day passes without some opportunity to do so.

Does charity require that you live with your father or mother in order to support them? Then keep up your love and affection for a life retired from the world, and do not attach your heart to your father's house more than is necessary to do what charity orders. Because of your station in life, is it inexpedient for you to keep perfect chastity? Then guard at least as much of it as you can without violating charity. Let him who cannot do the whole do some part of it.

You are not obliged to seek out a man who has injured you; it is his duty to return to himself and come and make amends to you since he went before you in the way of injury and insult. At the same time, Theotimus, go and do what the Savior counsels you to do: anticipate him in doing good, render him good for evil, cast on his head and heart burning coals as testimony of that charity which will inflame him through and through and compel him to love you.[82]

You are not obliged in strict law to give to all the poor you meet, but only to those who have very great need for help. But for all that, do not refuse to follow the Savior's counsel, and to all the needy you meet give willingly, as far as your condition and the true demands of your own affairs permit. You are not obliged to make any vow whatsoever, but make such as your spiritual director judges suitable for your advancement in God's love. You are free to use wine within the limits of propriety; however, in keeping with St. Paul's counsel to

[82] Rom. 12:20-21.

Timothy, take only as much as is necessary for your stomach's sake.[83]

In the counsels there are different degrees of perfection. To *lend* to the poor who are not in extreme need is the first degree of the counsel to give alms. A higher degree is to *give* to them, and one higher still is to *give them all you have*. Finally, it is the highest degree to give one's own self by dedicating it to the service of the poor. Apart from cases of extreme necessity, hospitality is a counsel. To entertain strangers is its first degree. To go out on the highways and invite them in, as Abraham did,[84] is a higher degree. It is still higher to live in dangerous places in order to rescue, help, and serve passersby.

That great saint Bernard of Menthon,[85] a native of this diocese, excelled in this counsel. He came from a very illustrious family, but he lived for many years among the cliffs and peaks of our Alps and there gathered together many companions in order to wait for, lodge, assist, and rescue travelers and passersby from the dangers of storms. Often such men would have died amid the tempest, snow, and cold, were it not for the hospices this great friend of God had founded and built on the two mountains which, for this very hospitality of his, are called by his name: Great St. Bernard, in the diocese of Sion, and Little St. Bernard, in that of Tarentaise.

To visit the sick who are not in extreme need is a praiseworthy work of charity, and to serve them is better still. But to

---

[83] 1 Tim. 5:23.

[84] Gen. 18:2-5.

[85] St. Bernard of Montjoux, also known as St. Bernard of Menthon (died 1081), founder of the two celebrated hospices of the Great and Little St. Bernard in the Alps.

dedicate one's self to their service is the perfection of that counsel. By their institute, the Clerics of the Visitation of the Sick do this, as do many women in various places. This is done in imitation of the great St. Samson,[86] a Roman gentleman and physician, who became a priest in Constantinople. There he devoted himself wholly and with wonderful charity to the service of the sick in a hospital founded by him, which the Emperor Justinian[87] built and finished. It is also in imitation of St. Catherine of Genoa[88] and St. Catherine of Siena,[89] of St. Elizabeth of Hungary,[90] and of those glorious friends of God St. Francis[91] and the Blessed Ignatius of Loyola,[92] who, at the beginning of their orders, carried out this work with incomparable fervor and spiritual profit.

The virtues have a certain range of perfection, and ordinarily we are not obliged to practice them in their highest degree of excellence. It is enough to enter so far into the exercise of them as to be actually engaged in it. To pass beyond this and advance in perfection is a counsel. Ordinarily, heroic acts of virtue are not commanded but only counseled. If we find on some occasion that we are obliged to practice them, this

---

[86] St. Samson (c. 490-565), Bishop of Dol.

[87] Justinian I (483-565), Roman emperor from 527.

[88] St. Catherine of Genoa (1447-1510), mystic.

[89] St. Catherine of Siena (c. 1347-1380), Dominican tertiary.

[90] St. Elizabeth of Hungary (1207-1231), wife of Ludwig IV and benefactress of the poor.

[91] St. Francis of Assisi (c. 1181-1226), founder of the Franciscan Order.

[92] St. Ignatius Loyola (1491-1556), founder of the Society of Jesus.

happens because of rare and extraordinary occurrences rendering such acts necessary to keep God's grace.

The blessed doorkeeper of the Sebaste prison saw one of the forty men then being martyred lose courage and the crown of martyrdom, and took his place — although no one had hunted him out — and thus became the fortieth of those glorious and triumphant soldiers of our Lord.[93] When St. Adauctus saw St. Felix[94] led to martyrdom, he said — even though no one urged him on — "I, too, am a Christian like him, and I adore the same Savior." Then he kissed St. Felix, walked with him to martyrdom, and was beheaded.

Thousands of ancient martyrs did the same thing. They were equally able to avoid or to submit to martyrdom without sin, but they chose generously to submit to martyrdom rather than lawfully to evade it. Therefore, for them, martyrdom was a heroic act of fortitude and constancy, which a holy excess of love granted them. But when it is necessary either to endure martyrdom or to renounce the Faith, martyrdom does not cease to be martyrdom and an excellent act of fortitude and love. Still I do not know if it must be called a heroic act, since it is not chosen by any excess of love, but by necessity imposed by the law commanding it in such cases.

The practice of acts of heroic virtue constitutes perfect imitation of the Savior, who, as the great St. Thomas says, had

---

[93] The forty martyrs of Sebaste (died c. 320) were Christian soldiers who, in Lesser Armenia during the Licinian persecution, were left naked on a frozen pond to die, with tubs of hot water on the pond's banks as a temptation to renounce their Faith.

[94] St. Adauctus and St. Felix (died c. 304), martyrs.

all the virtues in a heroic degree from the instant of His conception.[95] Indeed, I would prefer to call it more than heroic, since He was not simply more than man but infinitely more than man — that is, true God.

∞

Be open to God's inspirations
The sun's rays give light while giving warmth and warmth while giving light. Inspiration is a heavenly ray that brings into our hearts a warm light that makes us see the good, and fires us on to its pursuit. All that lives upon earth is dulled by the winter's cold, but with the return of vital heat in the springtime, all things get back their movement. Ground animals run more swiftly; birds fly higher and sing more gaily; plants more pleasingly put forth their leaves and flowers. Without inspiration our souls would live idle, sluggish, useless lives, but with the coming of the divine rays of inspiration, we feel a light mingled with a life-giving warmth that enlightens our understanding and awakens and animates our will by giving it the strength to will and do the good that pertains to eternal salvation.

When God had formed the human body out of "the slime of the earth," as Moses says, "He breathed into it the breath of life, and man was made into a living soul"[96] — that is, into a soul which gave life, movement, and activity to the body. This same eternal God breathes and infuses into our souls the inspirations of supernatural life to the end, as says the great apostle,

[95] St. Thomas Aquinas, *Summa Theologica*, III, Q. 7, art. 2, 12.
[96] Cf. Gen. 2:7.

that they may become "a life-giving spirit"[97] — that is, a spirit that makes us live, move, feel, and work the works of grace. Hence He who has given us being also gives us operation.

Man's breath warms things it enters into: witness the Shunammite woman's child, upon whose mouth the prophet Elisha placed his own mouth and breathed upon him, and his flesh grew warm.[98] Experience makes this warming power evident. But with regard to God's breath, not only does it warm, but it gives perfect light, since His divine Spirit is an infinite light. His vital breath is called inspiration because by it, supreme goodness breathes upon us and inspires in us the desires and intentions of His heart.

The means of inspiration that God uses are infinite. St. Anthony,[99] St. Francis, St. Anselm,[100] and a thousand others often received inspirations from the sight of creatures. Preaching is the ordinary means of inspiration. However, men whom the Word does not help are taught by tribulation, according to the words of the prophet, "And affliction shall give understanding of what you hear."[101] That is, those who hear God's threats against the wicked and do not correct themselves shall learn the truth by the result and effects and shall become wise by feeling affliction. St. Mary of Egypt[102] was inspired by the sight

---

[97] Cf. 1 Cor. 15:45.

[98] 4 Kings 4:34 (RSV = 2 Kings 4:34).

[99] St. Anthony of Egypt (c. 251-356), father of desert monasticism.

[100] Probably St. Anselm (c. 1033-1109), Archbishop of Canterbury. — ED.

[101] Cf. Isa. 28:19.

[102] St. Mary of Egypt, fifth-century woman who fled to the desert to do penance after a life of infamy as an actress and courtesan.

of an image of our Lady; St. Anthony, by hearing the Gospel
read at Mass; St. Augustine,[103] by hearing an account of St.
Anthony's life; the Duke of Gandia,[104] by seeing the dead em-
press; St. Pachomius,[105] by seeing an example of charity; the
Blessed Ignatius of Loyola, by reading the lives of the saints.
St. Cyprian[106] — this is not the great Bishop of Carthage but
another who was a glorious martyr — was touched by seeing
the Devil admit his impotence over those who trust in God.

When I was a youth in Paris, two students, one of whom was
a heretic, heard the bell for matins sound in the Carthusian
monastery after they had passed a night of debauchery in the
Faubourg St. Jacques. When the heretic asked why the bell
was ringing, his companion told him of the devotion with
which monks celebrated the sacred office in that holy monastery. "O God," he said, "how different is the conduct of those
religious from our own! They perform the office of angels,
while we perform that of beasts!"

He desired the next day to see by experience what he had
learned from his companion's account, and found those fathers
in their stalls, standing like marble statues in a row of niches,
motionless, devoid of all movement but that of chanting the
Psalms, which they did with truly angelic attention and devotion as is the custom of their holy order. The result was that

[103]St. Augustine (354-430), Bishop of Hippo.
[104]St. Francis Borgia (1510-1572), Duke of Gandia and Jesuit.
[105]St. Pachomius (c. 290-346), founder of Christian communal monasticism.
[106]St. Cyprian, converted magician of Antioch who was beheaded during the persecution by Diocletian in the early
fourth century.

that poor youth was completely carried away with admiration and was filled with the greatest consolation at seeing God so well adored among Catholics. He resolved, and afterward put it into effect, to place himself in the bosom of the Church, the true and unique spouse of Him who had sent His inspiration even to the infamous litter of abomination where He had lain.

Oh, how happy are they who keep their hearts open to holy inspirations! They never lack the graces necessary to them in order to live well and devoutly according to their conditions, and to fulfill in a holy way the duties of their professions. Just as God, by the ministry of nature, gives to each animal instincts needed for its preservation and the exercise of its natural properties, so too, if we do not resist God's grace, He gives to each of us the inspirations needed to live, work, and preserve ourselves in the spiritual life.

"Ah, Lord," said the faithful Eliezer, "Behold, I stand here at this spring of water, and the daughters of the inhabitants of this city will come out to draw water. Therefore, the maid to whom I shall say, 'Let down the pitcher that I may drink,' and she shall answer, 'Drink, and I will water your camels also,' she it is whom you have chosen for your servant Isaac."[107] Theotimus, Eliezer does not express any desire for water except for himself, but the fair Rebecca was obedient to the inspiration that God and her own kindness gave her and also offered water to his camels.[108] For this deed she was made the spouse of holy Isaac, fair daughter of the great Abraham, and ancestral mother of the Savior.

[107]Cf. Gen. 24:12-14.
[108]Gen. 24:17-19.

Souls not content merely with doing what the Divine Spouse requires of them by His commandments and counsels, but who are prompt to follow sacred inspirations, are truly those whom the eternal Father has prepared to be spouses of His beloved Son. With regard to the good Eliezer, since he could not otherwise distinguish among the daughters of Haran — that is, the town of Nahor — which one among them was destined for his master's son, God enabled him to recognize her by means of inspiration. When we do not know what to do and men's help is lacking to us in our perplexities, then God inspires us. If we are humbly obedient, He does not permit us to fall into error. I will say no more of ordinary inspirations, since I have spoken of them frequently both in this work and also in the *Introduction to the Devout Life*.[109]

---

[109]See *Introduction to the Devout Life*, Part 2, ch. 18.

Chapter Three

Follow God's will
in making decisions

៚

There are certain inspirations that tend solely to extraordinary perfection in the ordinary exercises of a Christian life. Charity toward the sick is an ordinary exercise among true Christians, but it was an ordinary exercise practiced with extraordinary perfection by St. Francis and St. Catherine of Siena — when they kissed the sores of lepers and the cancerous — and also by that glorious king St. Louis,[110] when with bare head, and on his knees, he served the sick. Because of this, a certain Cistercian abbot was completely lost in admiration as he saw the king in this posture handle and tend an unfortunate man, ulcered over with horrible, cancerous sores. It was also a most extraordinary exercise of that holy monarch to serve the most lowly and abject among the poor at his own table and to eat the remains of their food. In his hospital at Bethlehem, St. Jerome entertained pilgrims from Europe who had fled from the persecution of the Goths. He not only washed their feet, but even abased himself to wash and rub the legs of their camels after the example of Rebecca — whom we have just mentioned — who drew water not only for Eliezer, but for his camels as well.[111]

---

[110] St. Louis IX (1214-1270), king of France.
[111] Gen. 24:14.

Finding God's Will for You

St. Francis was very strict, not only in the practice of poverty, but also of simplicity. Once he bought a lamb that he was
afraid would be slaughtered, since it represented our Lord. He
showed respect for almost all creatures, since by an exceptional
but very prudent simplicity he contemplated in them their
Creator. Sometimes he would busy himself with removing
worms from the road so that no one would trample on them
when passing by,[112] for he recalled that his Savior compared
Himself to a worm.[113] By reason of a certain admirable consideration suggested to him by holy love, he called creatures his
brothers and sisters. St. Alexis,[114] a lord of very noble extrac-
tion, practiced self-abjection in an excellent way by living unknown in the house of his own father in Rome for seventeen
years in the guise of a poor pilgrim.

∞

Avoid undertaking too many
spiritual works at once

All these inspirations were for ordinary exercises practiced
with extraordinary perfection. In inspirations of this kind, we
should observe the rules for desires that we have given in our
Introduction.[115] We should not want to practice many exercises
at the same time and all of a sudden. The enemy often tries to

---

[112]Thomas of Celano (c. 1190-1260; Franciscan monk and earli-
est biographer of St. Francis of Assisi), *Legenda antiqua s.
Francisci*, Bk. 1, ch. 9-10.

[113]Cf. Ps. 21:7 (RSV = Ps. 22:6.

[114]St. Alexis, fifth-century nobleman who renounced his heri-
tage to become a beggar; also known as the Man of God.

[115]See *Introduction to the Devout Life*, Part 3, ch. 37.

make us attempt and start many projects so that we will be overwhelmed with too many tasks, and therefore achieve nothing and leave everything unfinished. Sometimes he even suggests the wish to undertake some excellent work that he foresees we will never accomplish. This is to distract us from the prosecution of some less excellent work that we would have easily completed. He does not care how many plans and beginnings we make, provided nothing is finished. No more than Pharaoh does he wish to prevent the "mystical women of Israel" — that is, Christian souls — from bringing forth male children, provided they are slain before they grow up.[116]

On the contrary, as the great St. Jerome says, "Among Christians it is not so much the beginning as the end that counts."[117] We must not swallow so much food that we cannot digest what we have taken. The spirit of the seducer holds us down to mere starts and keeps us content with a flowery springtime. The Spirit of God makes us consider beginnings only so as to arrive at the end, and makes us rejoice in the flowers of the spring only in expectation of enjoying the fruits of summer and autumn.

In the great St. Thomas's opinion, it is not expedient to consult much and deliberate long concerning an inclination to enter a good and well-regulated religious order.[118] He is right. Since the religious life is counseled by our Lord in the Gospel, what need is there for long consultation? It is sufficient to have one good discussion with a few people who are truly prudent and capable in such matters and able to help us come to a

[116] Cf. Exod. 1:16.

[117] St. Jerome, *Letter to Furia*, no. 6.

[118] St. Thomas Aquinas, *Summa Theologica*, II-II, Q. 189, art. 10.

short and solid solution to our problem. But as soon as we have deliberated and resolved — in this and in every other matter that concerns God's service, we must be firm and unchanging — we must never let ourselves be shaken by any show whatsoever of a greater good.

Very often, says the glorious St. Bernard, the evil one deludes us, and to distract us from achieving some good, he proposes another that seems better.[119] After we have started the second one, to divert us from completing it, he presents us with a third. He is satisfied if we make many beginnings, provided we never finish anything.

I borrow a good analogy from a letter of the great St. Anselm to Lanzon.[120] Just as a shrub that is often transplanted cannot take root and, as a result, cannot come to maturity and yield the desired fruit, so the soul that transplants its heart from plan to plan cannot profit or gain proper growth in perfection, since perfection does not consist in beginnings but in accomplishments. Ezekiel's sacred animals "went whither the impulse of the spirit led them, and they did not turn when they went" and "every one of them went straight forward."[121]

We, too, must go where inspiration impels us, neither turning around nor turning back, but without changing our gaze, marching on to where God has turned our face. If a man is on a good path, let him keep to it. Sometimes it happens that we forsake the good in order to seek the better, and while we leave the one, we do not find the other. Possession of a little treasure

---

[119]St. Bernard, *Sermones in Cantica*, nos. 9, 33.

[120]St. Anselm, *Epistola* 29.

[121]Ezek. 1:12.

actually found is worth more than expectation of a greater one we must still go out to seek. An inspiration urging us to give up some true good we already possess in order to pursue a future better good is suspect.

A young Portuguese man named Francis Bassus was admirable not only in sacred eloquence, but also in the practice of virtue, when under Blessed Philip Neri's[122] direction in the Roman Oratory. Then he believed that he was inspired to leave that holy society to join a formal religious order, and he finally resolved to do so. When Blessed Philip Neri assisted at his reception into the Order of St. Dominic, he wept bitterly. On being asked by Francis Mary Tauruse, later Archbishop of Siena and a cardinal, why he shed those tears, he said, "I deplore the loss of so many virtues." In fact, that young man who was so excellently prudent and devout in the congregation, after he entered the religious order became so inconstant and flighty that, agitated by various desires for novelty and change, he later caused great and grievous scandals.[123]

If a fowler goes straight to a partridge's nest, the bird will show herself to him and pretend to be weak and lame. She will rise up as if to make a great flight and then fall down all of a sudden as though unable to go any further. All this is done so that the hunter will keep after her, think he can catch her easily, and thus be distracted from finding her little ones outside the nest. When he has chased her for a while and fancies he has caught her, she takes to the air and escapes.

---

[122] St. Philip Neri (1515-1595), "Apostle of Rome," and founder of the Congregation of the Oratory.

[123] See Antonius Gallonius, *Life of Philip Neri* (Rome: 1600), ch. 6.

Thus, too, when our enemy sees a man who by God's inspiration undertakes a profession and way of life suitable to his advancement in heavenly love, he persuades him to take some other path, apparently of greater perfection. Having once lured the man from his first path, little by little he makes it impossible for him to follow the second. Next he proposes a third way to the man. All this is so that by busying himself with a continual search for different new ways to perfect himself, he is kept from using any and consequently from arriving at the end for which he seeks them — namely, perfection.

Young dogs at every turning leave the pack and change directions; wise old dogs never make any change but always follow the track they are on. Therefore, once we have found God's most holy will in our vocation, let each one of us devoutly and lovingly abide by it, and practice its proper exercises according to the order of discretion, and with zeal for perfection.

∞

Follow only those inspirations that are
holy and that bring your soul peace

Therefore, Theotimus, we must thus conduct ourselves in those inspirations which are extraordinary only in that they arouse us to practice a Christian's ordinary exercises with extraordinary fervor and perfection. But there are other exercises that are called extraordinary not only because they make the soul advance beyond the ordinary rate, but also because they carry it on to actions contrary to the common laws, rules, and customs of holy Church, and hence are worthy of admiration rather than imitation.

Follow God's will in making decisions

The holy maiden called by historians Eusebia the Stranger[124] left Rome, her native city, dressed as a boy, together with two other girls. They boarded a ship to go overseas, went to Alexandria and from there to the island of Cos. When Eusebia saw that it was safe to do so, she again put on the garments of her own sex, set out to sea again, and went over to Caria to the town of Mylasa, where the great St. Paul, who had found her in Cos and taken her under his spiritual guidance, brought her. After he had been made a bishop, he directed her so piously that she founded a monastery there and set herself to the Church's service in the office of deaconess, as it was then called. She did this with such charity that, in the end, she died a great saint and was recognized as such from the many miracles God wrought by her relics and through her intercession. To put on the garb of the opposite sex and, thus disguised, to expose herself to a voyage with men is not only beyond but against the ordinary rules of Christian modesty.

A young man who had kicked his mother was touched with lively repentance and went to confession to St. Anthony of Padua. To impress more vividly on him the horror of his sin, the saint said among other things to him, "My child, the foot that served as instrument of your malice deserves to be cut off!" The young man took this so seriously that when he went back to his mother's home, he was swept away by feelings of contrition and he cut off the foot. The saint's words would not have had such force, according to their usual meaning, unless

[124]See Simeon Metaphraste Logothetes, *Vita et conversatio sanctae Eusebiae, quae cognominata est Hospita, die 25 januarii*. Also Laurentius Surius, *De probatis sanctorum vitis* (Cologne: 1617), 414-417.

God added His inspiration to it. It was so extraordinary an inspiration that we would regard it rather as a temptation, unless the miraculous reunion of the amputated foot, effected through the saint's blessing, had given approval to it.[125]

St. Paul, the first hermit,[126] St. Anthony,[127] and St. Mary of Egypt did not bury themselves in those vast desert solitudes, deprived of hearing Mass, receiving Communion, and going to Confession — deprived too, young as they still were, of direction and all assistance — without powerful inspiration. The great St. Simeon Stylites led a life that no one in this world would even have thought of or undertaken without heavenly prompting and assistance. St. John, surnamed the Silent,[128] a bishop, forsook his diocese unknown to all his clergy and went to pass the rest of his days in the monastery of Laura without their having any further report of him. Was not this contrary to the rules that his holy residence be maintained?

The great St. Paulinus[129] sold himself in order to ransom a poor widow's son. How could he do this according to ordinary laws, since by episcopal consecration, he was not his own property, but belonged to his Church and to the people? As for those young girls and women who were pursued because of their beauty and therefore willfully disfigured their faces with

---

[125] See *Book of Miracles of St. Anthony*, ch. 4.

[126] St. Paul of Thebes (died c. 340).

[127] Probably St. Anthony of Egypt. — ED.

[128] St. John the Silent (454-558), Bishop of Colonia and later hermit.

[129] Possibly Bishop of Nola (c. 353-431); Trier (died 358); York (died 644); or Aquileia (c. 726-802). — ED.

wounds in order to guard their chastity under the show of a holy deformity: did they not do a thing apparently forbidden?

One of the best marks of the goodness of all inspirations and especially the extraordinary is peace and tranquillity of heart in those who receive them, since the Holy Spirit is indeed violent but with a violence that is gentle, mild, and peaceful. He comes "like a violent wind"[130] and like thunder from Heaven, but He does not overthrow them, nor does He trouble them. The fear seizing them at His sound is momentary and is immediately followed by a sweet assurance. For this reason the fire sits "on each of them,"[131] as if finding and also giving there its sacred repose.

Just as in the Song of Solomon the Savior is called a peaceful or pacific Solomon, so is His spouse called the Shulammite, the calm daughter of peace. The voice of the Spouse, that is, His inspiration, in no way disturbs or troubles her, but draws her so gently that He causes her soul to melt with delight and, as it were, to flow into Him. "My soul melted when my beloved spoke."[132] Although she is combative and warlike, yet at the same time she is so peaceful that amid armies and battles she keeps up the harmony of an unequaled melody. "What shall you see in the Shulammite but the choirs of armies?"[133] she asks. Her armies are choirs, that is, singers in harmony, and her choirs are armies, because the weapons of the Church and of the devout soul are naught else but prayers, hymns, canticles,

---

[130]Cf. Acts 2:2.

[131]Cf. Acts 2:3.

[132]Cf. Cant. 5:6 (RSV = Song of Sol. 5:6).

[133]Cf. Cant. 7:1 (RSV = Song of Sol. 6:14).

and psalms. Thus God's servants who have had the highest and most exalted inspirations have been the gentlest and most peaceable men in all the world. Such were Abraham, Isaac, and Jacob. Moses is called "a man exceedingly meek above all men."[134] David is praised for his mildness.[135]

On the contrary, the evil spirit is turbulent, bitter, and restless. Those who follow his hellish suggestions in the belief that they are heavenly inspirations can usually be recognized because they are unsettled, headstrong, haughty, and ready to undertake or meddle in affairs. Under the pretext of zeal, they subvert everything, criticize everyone, rebuke everyone, and find fault with everything. They are men without self-control and without consideration, who put up with nothing. In the name of zeal for God's honor, they indulge in the passions of self-love.

∞

*When following inspirations, always
obey the authority of the Church*

Most holy humility is inseparably joined to peace and joy of heart. I do not give the name humility to the ceremonious mixture of words, gestures, kissings of earth, signs of reverence, and bows, if these are made, as often happens, without any inward sense of one's own abjection, and lack true esteem for our neighbor. All that is merely the vain amusement of feeble minds. It must be called phantom humility rather than humility itself. I speak here of noble, genuine, fruitful, solid

[134]Num. 12:3.
[135]Cf. Ps. 131:1 (RSV = Ps. 132:1).

humility, which makes us easy to correct, submissive, and prompt to obey.

While the incomparable Simeon Stylites was still a novice at Teleda,[136] he refused to respond to the advice of his superiors who wished to keep him from practicing the many strange forms of austerity he observed with inordinate severity. For this reason he was expelled from the monastery as a man not very susceptible to mortification of heart and much given to that of the body. Afterward he came to his senses, became more devout and wiser in the spiritual life, and behaved quite differently, as is proved by the following event.

When the hermits who were scattered about the desert regions near Antioch learned of the extraordinary life he led on his pillar, where he seemed to be either an angel on earth or a man from Heaven, they sent him a representative whom they instructed to speak for them in the following fashion: "Simeon, why have you left the great path of the devout life, trodden by so many great and holy predecessors, and followed another path unknown to men and far distant from everything seen or heard of up to the present? Simeon, get down from that pillar, and join the others in the way of life and method of serving God used by those good fathers who were our predecessors."

In the event that Simeon agreed with their advice and showed himself ready and willing to descend from his pillar so as to condescend to their will, the hermits had instructed their messenger to leave him free to persevere in the kind of life he had begun. By such obedience, those good fathers said, they

---

[136] A monastery in Syria.

could easily recognize that he had entered this kind of life under divine inspiration. On the contrary, if he resisted, despised their exhortation, and wished to follow his own will, then they resolved that it would be necessary to take him down by force and make him give up his pillar.

When the deputy had arrived at the pillar, he had no sooner announced his mission than the great Simeon without delay, without reservation, and without any reply, started to descend with obedience and humility worthy of his rare sanctity. When the delegate saw this, he said, "Simeon, stop and stay there, persevere with constancy, and have good courage. Follow valiantly your enterprise. Your sojourn on that pillar is from God."[137]

Theotimus, I implore you to observe carefully how those holy anchorites of old in general meeting found no surer mark of heavenly inspiration in a matter so extraordinary as the life of St. Stylites than to see that he was simple, gentle, and tractable under the laws of most holy obedience. God blessed the submission of that great man and gave him the grace to persevere for thirty whole years upon a column more than fifty feet high, after having previously passed seven years on other columns six, twelve, and twenty feet high, and having been ten years on a little rocky point in a place called the Mandra.[138] Thus this bird of paradise, living in air and not touching earth, was a spectacle of love for angels and of admiration for men. In obedience, everything is safe; apart from obedience, all is subject to suspicion.

[137]Cf. Theodoretus, *Historia religiosa*, ch. 26, Nicephorus Callistus, *Ecclesiastica historia*, Bk. 14, ch. 51.
[138]A mountain in Syria.

Follow God's will in making decisions

When God sends His inspirations into a man's heart, the first one He gives is that of obedience. Was there ever a clearer and more striking inspiration than that given to the glorious St. Paul? Its chief point was that he should go into the city where he would learn from Ananias's lips what he himself was to do.[139] This Ananias was a very celebrated man and, as St. Dorotheus[140] says, bishop of Damascus. A man who says that he is inspired and then refuses to obey his superiors and follow their advice is an impostor. All prophets and preachers inspired by God have always loved the Church, always adhered to Her doctrine, and always had Her approval. They have never proclaimed anything as forcefully as this truth, that "the lips of the priest shall keep knowledge," and that they must "seek the law at his mouth."[141]

Hence extraordinary missions are diabolical illusions and not heavenly inspirations if they are not recognized and approved by pastors on the ordinary mission. In this, Moses and the prophets are in accord. St. Francis, St. Dominic,[142] and the other fathers of religious orders turned to the service of souls by an extraordinary inspiration, but they submitted all the more humbly and heartily to the sacred hierarchy of the Church. To sum up, the three best and surest marks of lawful inspiration are perseverance in contrast to inconstancy and levity, peace and gentleness of heart in contrast to disquiet

---

[139] Acts 9:7.

[140] St. Dorotheus (sixth-century ascetical writer), *De septuaginta domini discipulis*, ch. 8, n. 5.

[141] Mal. 2:7.

[142] St. Dominic (1170-1221), founder of the Order of Friars Preachers.

and solicitude, and humble obedience in contrast to obstinacy and extravagance.

We conclude all we have said concerning the union of our will with God's signified will. Almost all herbs with yellow flowers, and even wild chicory, which has blue flowers, always turn toward the sun and follow its course. But the sunflower turns not only its flowers, but all its leaves to follow that great luminary. In the same manner, all the elect turn their heart's flower — namely, obedience to the commandments — toward the divine will.

However, souls entirely caught up in holy love do not merely look toward this divine goodness by their obedience to the commandments, but do more than that. By the union of all their affections without any reserve or exception whatsoever, they follow the course of that divine sun in all that it commands, counsels, and inspires them to do. Therefore, they can say with the sacred psalmist: "Lord, You have held my right hand, and You have guided me in Your will, and with much glory You have received me. I have become like a horse in Your presence, and I am always with You."[143] For just as a well-trained horse is managed easily, gently, and properly in all situations by his rider, so also a soul that loves is so pliable under God's will that He does in it all He wishes.

∞

Avoid being anxious about little things
St. Basil says that when God's will is shown clearly to us by His ordinances and commandments, there is nothing further

to deliberate on, for we must simply do what has been ordained.[145] But for all other things, it is in our liberty to choose what seems good according to our preferences, although we must not do all that is lawful, but only what is expedient. Finally, he says, to determine properly what is suitable, we must listen to the advice of a wise spiritual director.

I must warn you, Theotimus, against a troublesome temptation that sometimes comes to souls who have a great desire to follow in all things what best accords with God's will. On every occasion the enemy puts them in doubt as to whether it is God's will for them to do one thing rather than another. For example, they ask whether it is God's will for them to dine with a certain friend or not to dine with him; whether they should wear gray clothes or black; whether they should fast on Friday or Saturday; or whether they should take some recreation or abstain from it. In this way they waste a great deal of time. While busying and perplexing themselves to discover what is better, they needlessly lose opportunities to do many good deeds. The accomplishment of such deeds would be more to God's glory than this distinction between the good and the better — with which they have amused themselves — could ever be.

It is not common practice to weigh small coins, but only pieces of value. Business transactions would be too troublesome and consume too much time if we had to weigh pennies, halfpence, farthings, and half-farthings. In like manner, we do not have to weigh all kinds of little actions to learn if some have greater value than others. Frequently there is even a

---

[145]St. Basil the Great (c. 330-379; one of the three Cappadocian Fathers), Moralia, rules 9, 12, 33.

certain superstition in wanting to make such an examination. To what purpose should we trouble ourselves as to whether it is better to hear Mass in one church rather than in another, to spin rather than sew, or to give alms to a man rather than to a woman?

It is not giving good service to a master to spend as much time thinking about what is to be done as in doing what is required. We should measure out our attention according to the importance of what we undertake. It would be ill-ordered care to take as much trouble over planning a day's journey as over one of three or four hundred leagues.

Choice of vocation, plans for some affair of great importance, a work requiring a long time or some very great expenditure of money, change of residence, choice of associates, and such similar things require that we think seriously as to what best accords with God's will. But in little daily actions, in which even a mistake is neither of consequence, nor beyond repair, what need is there for us to make a great to-do, give them much attention, and stop to make importunate consultations with others? To what purpose will I make trouble for myself to learn whether God prefers me to say the Rosary or the Office of Our Lady? There can be no such great differences between the one and the other that a long inquest should be held.

So also as to such things as the following: Should I go to the hospital to visit the sick rather than to vespers? Should I go to hear a sermon rather than visit a church where I could gain an indulgence? Ordinarily there is nothing of such obvious importance in one rather than the other that there is need to go into long deliberation over it. We must proceed in good faith

Follow God's will in making decisions

and without making subtle distinctions in such affairs and, as St. Basil says, do freely what seems good to us, so as not to weary our minds, waste our time, and put ourselves in danger of disquiet, scruples, and superstition — that is, when there is no great disproportion between one work and another and where we meet no important circumstances on one side rather than the other.

Even in important matters, we must be very humble and not think of finding God's will by force of scrutiny and subtle discussion. After we have implored the light of the Holy Spirit, applied our thought to search for His good pleasure, taken counsel with our director and perhaps with two or three other spiritual persons, we must come to a resolution and decision in the name of God. After that we must not call our choice in doubt, but devoutly, peacefully, and firmly keep and sustain it.

Although the difficulties, temptations, and different events that occur in the course of carrying out our plan may cause us some uncertainty as to whether we have chosen well, still we must remain firm and not consider all such things. Rather, we must reflect that if we had made some other choice, we might be a hundred times worse off, and furthermore that we do not know if God wills us to be trained in consolation or in desolation, in peace or in war. Once our resolution has been devoutly made, we must never doubt the holiness of its execution. If we do not fail, it cannot fail. To act otherwise is a mark of great self-love, or of childishness, weakness, and folly of mind.

Chapter Four

Learn to embrace
your crosses

Sin excepted, nothing is done except by what is called God's absolute will or the will of good pleasure. No one can block this will. It is known to us only by its effects. When they are accomplished, they make clear to us the fact that God has willed and planned them.

Theotimus, let us consider as a sum total all that has been, is, and shall be. Completely rapt in amazement, we shall then be forced to cry out in imitation of the psalmist, "I will praise You because You are excessively magnified. Wonderful are Your works, and my soul knew this full well. Your knowledge is too wonderful to me. It is too lofty for me to attain."[146] From there we will pass on to a most holy complacence, rejoicing because God is so infinite in wisdom, power, and goodness, the three divine properties of which the universe is but a small proof and, as it were, a sample.

Let us review both men and angels and that whole varied array of nature, qualities, conditions, powers, affections, passions, graces, and privileges which supreme Providence has established in the countless multitude of those celestial intelligences and human persons in whom divine justice and

[146]Cf. Ps. 138:14, 6 (RSV = Ps. 139:14, 6).

mercy are so wonderfully exercised. We shall be unable to keep ourselves from singing with joy filled with respect and loving fear: "All honor, Lord, to Your just law I bring; Your mercy and Your righteousness I sing."[147]

∞

Be assured that God's will for
you is both just and merciful

Theotimus, we must take the greatest complacence as we see how God exercises His mercy by the many diverse favors He distributes among angels and men, in Heaven and on earth, and how He exercises His justice by an infinite variety of trials and punishments. His justice and His mercy are in themselves equally worthy of love and admiration, since both of them are simply one and the same most unique goodness and Godhead.

Because the effects of His justice are severe and full of bitterness for us, He always sweetens them by mingling among them the effects of His mercy. Amid the waters of the deluge of His just wrath He keeps safe the green olive, and He enables the devout soul, like a chaste dove,[148] to find it at last if it will only lovingly meditate in the manner of doves.[149] Hence death, affliction, sweat, and toil, with which life abounds, are by God's just decree punishments for sin, but they are also by His sweet mercy ladders to ascend to Heaven, means to increase in grace, and merits to obtain glory. Blessed are poverty, hunger, thirst,

---

[147]Cf. Ps. 100:1 (RSV = Ps. 101:1).
[148]Gen. 8:10-11.
[149]Isa. 38:14.

sorrow, sickness, death, and persecution.[150] They are in truth just punishments for our faults, but they are punishments so steeped and, as the physicians say, so aromatized in God's sweetness, benignity, and mercy that theirs is a most pleasant bitterness.

Theotimus, it is a thing strange yet true that if the damned were not blinded by their obstinacy and hatred for God, they would find consolation in their torments and see how wonderfully divine mercy is mingled with the flames that eternally consume them. Hence when the saints contemplate on one hand the horrible and fearsome torments of the damned, they praise God's justice and cry out, "In You alone has justice reigned, and still, impartial law flows from Your mighty will."[151]

On the other hand, they see that although such torments are eternal and incomprehensible, they are still far less than the faults and crimes for which they have been indicted. Hence they are enraptured by God's infinite mercy and say, "Will God then cast us off forever? Or will He never be more favorable again? Or will He cut off His mercy forever, from generation to generation? Or will God forget to show mercy? Or will He in His anger shut up His mercies?"[152]

Lastly, let us turn to ourselves in particular and see both the quantity of interior and exterior goods and the very great number of interior and exterior punishments that Divine Providence has prepared for us in most holy justice and mercy. As if opening the arms of our consent, let us most lovingly

[150]Cf. Matt. 5:3, 5-6, 10-11.
[151]Cf. Ps. 118:137 (RSV = Ps. 119:137).
[152]Cf. Ps. 76:8-10 (RSV = Ps. 77:8-10).

embrace all this as we acquiesce in God's most holy will, and let us sing to Him as a hymn of eternal acquiescence, "Your will be done, on earth as it is in Heaven."[153]

> *Yes, Lord, Your will be done, on earth where we have no pleasure without admixture of some pain, no roses without thorns, no day without a night to follow, no spring without a winter that went before; on earth, Lord, where consolations are rare and trials are countless. Still, O God, Your will be done, not only in the fulfillment of Your commandments, counsels, and inspirations, which must be done by us, but also in the suffering of afflictions and punishments, which must be accepted by us, to the end that by us, for us, in us, and with us, Your will may do all that is pleasing to it.*

∽

Recognize suffering as a sign of God's love

Considered in themselves, trials certainly cannot be loved, but looked at in their origin — that is, in God's Providence and ordaining will — they are worthy of unlimited love. Look at the rod of Moses as it lies on the ground; there it is a loathsome serpent. Look at it in Moses' hand; there it is a miraculous wand.[154] Tribulations considered in themselves are dreadful things; looked at in God's will, they are things of love and delight. Often have we felt disgust for remedies and medicines when a doctor or apothecary gives them to us, but when offered

[153]Matt. 6:10.
[154]Exod. 7:10, 20.

to us by some loved hand, love conquers our loathing and we take them with joy. In fact, love either removes the harsh character of suffering or makes pleasant our experience of it.[155]

It is said that in Bocotia there is a river in which the fishes seem to be made of gold, but when taken out of their native waters they have the same natural color as other fish.[156] Afflictions are like that. If we look at them apart from God's will, they are naturally bitter. If we consider them in that eternal good pleasure, we find them all gold and more lovely and precious than can be described. If the great Abraham had seen need to slay his son, entirely apart from the will of God, Theotimus, think of what pangs and convulsions of heart he would have suffered. When he sees God's good pleasure, it is pure gold to him and he embraces it tenderly. If the martyrs had looked at their torments apart from that good pleasure, how little would they have sung in irons and amid the flames! A truly loving heart loves God's good pleasure not only in consolations, but also in afflictions, but it loves it most of all in the cross, in pain, and labor, because love's principal power is to enable the lover to suffer for the beloved object.

The Stoics, particularly good Epictetus,[157] placed all their philosophy in this: to abstain and sustain; to forbear and to bear up under; to abstain from and to forbear earthly pleasures, delights, and honors, and to sustain and to bear up under injuries, labors, and troubles.[158] Christian doctrine, the sole true philosophy,

[155]See St. Augustine, *De bono viduitatis*, ch. 21.
[156]Pliny the Elder, *Natural History*, Bk. 2, ch. 106.
[157]Epictetus (c. 50-130), Stoic philosopher.
[158]Aulua Gellius, *Noctes atticae*, Bk. 19, ch. 5-6.

has three principles on which it bases all its practices: self-denial, which is far more than to abstain from pleasures; to carry Christ's cross, which is far more than to lift it up; and to follow our Lord, not only in renouncing self and in carrying His Cross, but also in whatever belongs to the practice of every kind of good work.[159] Still it is evident that there is not as much love in self-denial and such deeds as in suffering. In fact, in Sacred Scripture, the Holy Spirit points out that the climax in our Lord's love for us is the Passion and death He suffered for us.[160]

To love God's will in consolations is a good love when it is truly God's will we love and not the consolation wherein it lies. Still, it is a love without opposition, repugnance, or effort. Who would not love so worthy a will in so agreeable a form?

To love God's will in His commandments, counsels, and inspirations is the second degree of love and it is much more perfect. It carries us forward to renounce and give up our own will, and enables us to abstain from and forbear many pleasures, but not all of them.

To love suffering and affliction out of love for God is the summit of most holy charity. In it nothing is pleasant but the divine will alone; there is great opposition on the part of our nature; and not only do we forsake all pleasures, but we embrace torments and labors.

The malignant enemy knows well what is the last refinement of love. When he had heard from God's mouth that Job was "just, righteous, fearing God, avoiding evil,"[161] and firm in

[159]Matt. 10:38, 16:24.
[160]John 15:13; Rom. 5:8-9; 1 John 3:16.
[161]Cf. Job 1:1.

innocence, he deemed all this but a trifle in comparison with suffering under affliction, and by them he made the final and greatest trial of that great servant of God. To make those afflictions extremely severe, he fashioned them out of Job's loss of all his possessions and all his children, abandonment by all his friends, and arrogant opposition from his closest associates and his own wife. It was opposition filled with contempt, mockery, and reproach. To this Satan added a complex of almost all human maladies, particularly a general, excruciating, noisome, horrible ulcer.

Nevertheless, behold great Job! He is like a king among the unfortunate of the earth; he is seated upon a dunghill, as upon a throne of misery; he is adorned with sores, ulcers, and rottenness as with royal robes suitable to the quality of his kingship. Behold great Job as he cries out, "If we have received good things from the hand of the Lord, why shall we not receive evil things as well?"[162] These are the words of a mighty love!

Theotimus, Job reflects that it is from God's hand that he received those good things, thus testifying that he loved those goods not so much because they were good as because they had come from the hand of the Lord. Since this is so, he concludes that he must lovingly bear up under adversities because they come from the same hand of the Lord, which is equally kind when it apportions affliction and when it gives out consolations. Good things are willingly accepted by all men, but to accept evils belongs only to perfect love. Because evils are lovable only in respect to the hand that gives them, perfect love has so much the greater love for them.

[162]Cf. Job 2:10.

Finding God's Will for You

A traveler who fears that he has lost the right road walks on in doubt. As he goes, he looks at the countryside now here, now there, and worries and wonders at the end of almost every field whether he has not gone astray. The man who is sure of his route goes along cheerfully, confidently, and quickly. In like manner, love wishing to go forward according to God's will amid consolations always goes in fear. It is afraid of making a wrong turn, and instead of loving God's good pleasure, it loves only the particular pleasure found in the consolation. But if love takes its path straight through God's will amid affliction, it walks on with assurance. Since affliction is in no way lovable in itself, it is a very easy thing to love it solely in reference to the hand that gives it.

In springtime, hounds make mistakes at every turn and have almost no power to smell, as herbs and flowers then send forth so strong an odor that it overcomes that of the stag or hare. In the springtime of consolation, love has almost no recognition of God's good pleasure, since the sensible pleasure arising from consolation casts such allurements into the heart that it disturbs the attention it should give to God's will. After our Lord had offered St. Catherine of Siena the choice of a crown of gold or a crown of thorns, she chose the second as more in keeping with love. It is a sure mark of love, says the Blessed Angela of Foligno,[163] to desire to suffer. The great apostle cries out that he glories only in the Cross, in infirmity, in persecution.[164]

[163]Blessed Angela of Foligno (c. 1248-1309; Umbrian mystic); Amaldus of Foligno, *Beatae Angelae Fulginatis vita et opuscula* (Foligno: 1714), 225.

[164]Gal. 6:14.

Learn to embrace your crosses

∞

Resign yourself to God's will in sufferings

Love of the Cross makes us undertake voluntary afflictions, such as fasting, and makes us renounce pleasures, honors, and riches. The love found in such exercises is completely agreeable to the beloved. It is still more so when we patiently, gently, and contentedly accept pains, torments, and tribulations in consideration of God's will, which sends them to us. Love reaches its most exalted state when we accept afflictions not only easily and patiently, but even cherish, like, and embrace them because of that divine good pleasure from which they come.

Among all the efforts of perfect love, that effort made by acquiescence of spirit in spiritual tribulations is undoubtedly the purest and noblest. The Blessed Angela of Foligno gives an admirable description of the interior pains she sometimes experienced. Her soul, she says, was tortured "like a man who is bound hand and foot and hung by his neck and, although not strangled, remains in this state between life and death without hope of relief," unable either to stand on his feet or to help himself with his hands, unable to cry out or even to sigh or groan.[165]

The situation is this, Theotimus: at times the soul is so weighed down by interior afflictions that all its faculties and powers are oppressed by privation of whatever can give it joy and by apprehension and experience of all that can sadden it. Hence, in imitation of the Savior, the soul begins to be greatly

---

[165] Amaldus of Foligno, *Beatae Angelae Fulginatis vita et opuscula* (Foligno: 1714), 33-34.

troubled, to fear, to suffer dread, and finally to feel sad with a
sadness like that of the dying. Well can the soul say, "My soul
is sad, even unto death."[166] With the consent of all that is within
it, the soul desires, asks, and pleads, "If it is possible, let this
cup be removed."[167] Nothing is left to it but the supreme part of
the spirit,[168] which is attached to the heart and good pleasure
of God and says with most simple acquiescence, "Eternal Father, not my will but Yours be done."[169]

This is the important thing. The soul makes this act of resignation among so many troubles and amid such opposition
and repugnance that it scarcely perceives that it makes it. At
least it thinks it is done so feebly as not to be done sincerely or
properly. What occurs there for God's good pleasure is done
not only without pleasure and content, but against all pleasure
and content in all the rest of the heart. Yet love permits itself
to lament at least for the fact that it cannot lament, and to utter all the lamentations of Job and Jeremiah, but on condition

[166]Matt. 26:38; Mark 14:34.

[167]Cf. Matt. 26:39; Luke 22:42.

[168]Here, St. Francis refers to one part of the soul. In Book 1 of his
Treatise on the Love of God he distinguishes between the superior, or higher, part of the soul and the inferior, or lower, part:
"In our soul as rational we clearly see two degrees of perfection. . . . That which reasons and draws conclusions according
to what it learns and experiences by the senses is called the inferior part. That which reasons and draws conclusions according
to intellectual knowledge, not grounded on sense experience
but on the discernment and judgment of the spirit, is called
the superior part. The superior part is usually called spirit and
the mental part of the soul, while the inferior part is com-
monly called sense or feeling, and human reason," Bk. 1, ch.
11. — ED.

[169]Cf. Matt. 26:39; Luke 22:42.

that that sacred acquiescence is always made in the depths of the soul, in the supreme and most delicate part of the spirit.

Such acquiescence is neither tender nor sweet and hardly perceptible to the senses, although it is true, strong, invincible, and most loving. It seems to have retired back to the farthest end of the spirit as into a dungeon or fortress where it maintains its courage, although all the rest of the soul is seized and oppressed by sorrow. In this state, the more love is stripped of all help and abandoned by every assistance from the soul's powers and faculties, the more it is to be prized for so constantly preserving its fidelity.

This union and conformity with God's good pleasure is made by holy resignation or by most holy indifference. Resignation is practiced by way of effort and submission. We would much prefer to live rather than die, but since it is God's good pleasure that we die, we acquiesce in it. We would like to live, if that were pleasing to God — even more, we would like it to be pleasing to God to make us live. Yet we die with a sincere heart, even though we would more willingly remain alive. We depart with a sufficiently good will, but we would remain here even more gladly.

In his afflictions, Job made this act of resignation: "If we have received good things from the hands of God, why shall we not receive the pains and toils He sends to us?" Theotimus, note how Job speaks of sustaining, supporting, and enduring. "As it has pleased the Lord, so is it done: blessed be the name of the Lord."[170] These are words of resignation and acceptance by way of suffering and patience.

[170]Job 1:21.

∞

Cultivate a holy indifference to all but God's good pleasure

Resignation prefers God's will above all things, yet it does not cease to love many other things in addition to God's will. Holy indifference goes beyond resignation, for it loves nothing except for love of God's will, so that nothing touches the indifferent heart in the presence of God's will. It is true that even the most indifferent heart in the world can be touched by some affection as long as it does not yet know where God's will lies.

When Eliezer arrived at Haran's well, he saw the virgin Rebecca and undoubtedly found her "exceedingly fair" and lovely. However, he remained indifferent to her until he knew by the sign God revealed to him that the divine will had prepared her for his master's son. Thereupon he gave her "golden earrings and bracelets."[171] On the contrary, if all Jacob liked in Rachel was alliance with Laban, to which Isaac, his father, had bound him, he would have liked Leah just as much as Rachel, since one was just as much Laban's daughter as the other. As a result, his father's will would have been carried out in one as well as in the other. But because, in addition to his father's will, he desired to satisfy his own particular liking, since he was smitten by Rachel's beauty and gentleness, he did not want to marry Leah and took her reluctantly and with resignation.[172]

The indifferent heart is not like this. It knows that tribulation — even though ill-favored like another Leah — does not cease to be the daughter, the beloved daughter, of God's good

[171]Cf. Gen. 24:16-22.
[172]Gen. 29:16-30.

pleasure. It loves tribulation as much as consolation, although the latter is more agreeable in itself. It even has greater love for tribulation, because it sees in it nothing to be loved except the mark of God's will. If I like only pure water, what does it matter to me whether it is served in a goblet of gold or in one of glass, since in either case I drink only the water? In fact, I will prefer it in the glass, since the glass has the same color as the water, which I can thus see much better. What does it matter whether God's will is offered to me in tribulation or in consolation? In each of them, I neither desire nor seek anything except the divine will, which is better seen, because no other beauty is present there but that of God's most holy, eternal good pleasure.

Heroic, yes, more than heroic, is the indifference of St. Paul the incomparable. "I am hard pressed," he says to the Philippians, "from two sides, desiring to be delivered from this body and to be with Christ, a thing far better, and yet to remain in this life for your sake."[173] He was imitated in this by the great bishop St. Martin,[174] who, when he came to the end of his life and was pressed by an extreme desire to go to God, still testified that he would most willingly remain to carry out the tasks laid upon him for the good of his beloved flock. It was as if he had sung this canticle:

> *How beautiful to see Your shining courts,*
> *O Lord! How like are they to mighty forts*
> *Where dauntless angel hosts forever dwell*

[173]Cf. Phil. 1:23, 24.
[174]St. Martin of Tours (c. 316-397), Bishop of Tours and patron saint of France.

And ever sing unto Your holy name,
And raise up paeans to Your praise and fame,
Greater by far than mind and tongue can tell!
My soul and flesh leap up in 'raptured strife
To join that throng with You, O God of life![175]

Then he continued and cried out, "Nevertheless, Lord, if I am still needed to serve for the salvation of Your people, I do not refuse the labor. Your will be done!" Admirable is the indifference of the apostle; admirable that of this apostolic man! They see Paradise open to them; they see a thousand labors on earth. The choice of one or the other is indifferent to them.

Only God's will can give a counterweight to their hearts. Paradise is no more worthy of love than the miseries of this world if God's good pleasure lies equally in them both. For them to toil is Paradise, if God's will is found in it, whereas Paradise is a trial if God's will is not found in it. As David says, they ask for neither Heaven nor earth, but only to see God's good pleasure accomplished: "O Lord, what is there in Heaven for me, or what do I desire upon earth besides You?"[176]

The indifferent heart is like a ball of wax in God's hands, ready to receive all the impressions of His eternal good pleasure. It is a heart without choice, equally ready for all things and having no other object for its will except the will of God. It does not place its love in the things God wills, but in the will of God who wills them. Therefore, when God's will is

[175]Cf. Ps. 83:2-3 (RSV = Ps. 84:1-2).
[176]Cf. Ps. 72:25 (RSV = Ps. 73:25).

found in many things, the indifferent heart chooses, no matter what the cost may be, that in which more of God's will abides.

God's good pleasure is found in both marriage and virginity. However, because it is greater in virginity, the indifferent heart chooses virginity, even though it might cost its life. So it was with St. Thecla,[177] St. Paul's dear spiritual daughter, St. Cecilia, St. Agatha,[178] and a thousand others. God's will is found in serving both poor and rich, but a little more in service of the poor. The indifferent heart will choose the latter. God's will lies in exercising restraint amid consolations and in practicing patience in tribulation. The indifferent heart prefers the second because it contains more of God's will.

To sum up, God's good pleasure is the supreme object of the indifferent soul. Wherever it sees it, it runs after it "in the odor of His perfume."[179] Without consideration of anything else, the soul always searches for the place where there is more of God's will. The soul is led on by God's will as by a beloved chain, and wherever His will goes, the soul follows. It would prefer Hell with God's will to Paradise without God's will. Yes, it would prefer Hell to Paradise if it knew that it would find a little more of God's good pleasure in Hell than in Heaven. Therefore — to imagine something impossible — if the soul knew that damnation would be a little more pleasing to God than salvation, it would forsake salvation and run after its own damnation.

[177]St. Thecla, first-century Christian virgin.
[178]St. Agatha (dates unknown), virgin and martyr.
[179]Cf. Cant. 1:3 (RSV = Song of Sol. 1:4).

Finding God's Will for You

༉

Practice holy indifference in all aspects of your life

Holy indifference must be practiced in things that concern
natural life, such as health, sickness, beauty, ugliness, weakness, and strength; in things concerning civil life, such as honors, rank, and wealth; in the various aspects of the spiritual life,
such as dryness, consolation, delight, and aridity; and in actions, and in sufferings — in sum, in every event of every kind.

With regard to natural life, Job was covered over with the
most horrible sores that man had ever seen. With regard to
civil life, he was scorned, scoffed at, and vilified. With regard
to the spiritual life, he was overwhelmed with weakness, op-
pressive feelings, convulsions, anguish, gloom, and every kind
of intolerable interior sorrow, as his complaints and lamentations prove. The great apostle proclaims to us a general indifference, so that we show ourselves to be true "minsters of God,
in much patience, in tribulations, in hardships, in labors, in
sleepless nights, in fastings; in chastity, in knowledge, in long-
suffering, in kindness, in the Holy Spirit, in unaffected love;
in the word of truth, in the power of God; with the armor of
justice on the right hand and on the left; in honor and dishonor, in evil report and good report; as deceivers and yet
truthful; as unknown and yet well-known; as dying, and behold, we live; as chastised, but not killed; as sorrowful, yet always rejoicing; as poor, yet enriching many; as having nothing,
yet possessing all things."[180]

Note, I beg of you, Theotimus, how grievously the lives of
the apostles are afflicted: in the body by stripes, in the heart by

[180]Cf. 2 Cor. 6:4-10.

distress, and in the world by ill report and imprisonment. Amid all such things, what indifference is theirs! Their sorrow is joyous, their poverty rich, their death life-giving, and their dishonor honorable. That is, they are joyful at being sad, content with being poor, strengthened for life amid the dangers of death, and they glory at being reviled, because such is the will of God. Because God's will is recognized better in suffering than in acts of other virtues, St. Paul puts the exercise of patience in the first place, saying, "But in all things, let us exhibit ourselves as the ministers of God, in much patience, in tribulations, in hardships," and then at the end, "in chastity, in prudence, in long-suffering."

Thus our divine Savior was afflicted with incomparable woes in civil life: He was condemned as guilty of treason against God and man; He was beaten, scourged, reviled, and tortured with most extreme ignominy. In His natural life, He died in the most cruel and piercing torments we can imagine. In His spiritual life, He suffered sadness, fear, terror, anguish, abandonment, and inner depression as never had and never shall have an equal. For although the highest portion of His soul supremely rejoiced in eternal glory, love hindered this glory from extending its delights into His feelings, imagination, or lower reason, and thus left His entire heart exposed to sorrow and anguish.

Ezekiel saw "the likeness of a hand" which "seized him by a single lock of the hair of his head," and lifted him up between Heaven and earth.[181] Our Lord likewise was lifted up on the Cross between Heaven and earth, and seemed to be held by His Father's hand only by the highest part of His spirit, as it

---

[181]Cf. Ezek. 8:3.

were, by a single hair of His head, which was touched by the gentle hand of the eternal Father and received a supreme affluence of felicity. All the rest was swallowed up in grief and sorrow. For this reason He cries out, "My God, my God, why have You forsaken me?"[182]

It is said that in the midst of the tempest, the fish called the sea lantern thrusts its tongue above the waves and is so luminous, brilliant, and clear that it serves as a light or beacon for sailors.[183] So, too, in the sea of sufferings that overwhelmed our Lord, all the faculties of His soul were swallowed up and buried, as it were, in a maelstrom of fearful pain. The highest part of His spirit was alone excepted. Left exempt from all suffering, it was bright and resplendent with glory and joy. Oh, how blessed is the love that reigns within the faithful at the summit of their spirit while they are amid the surging waves of inward tribulation!

∞

Leave the success of your endeavors in God's hands

We would hardly recognize God's good pleasure apart from actual events. Hence as long as it is unknown to us, we must keep as close as possible to God's will as it is manifested or signified to us. But as soon as His divine majesty's good pleasure becomes evident, we must immediately place ourselves under His loving obedience.

Suppose I am ill in bed. How am I to know if it is God's will that death should come? Actually, I know nothing about it.

[182]Matt. 27:46.

[183]Pliny the Elder, *Natural History*, Bk. 9, ch. 43.

However, I am very sure that while I await the outcome that God's good pleasure has ordained, He wills by His declared will that I use remedies suitable to effect a cure. Hence I will do this faithfully, forgetting nothing of what I can properly contribute to this purpose. But if it is God's good pleasure that sickness should win out over such remedies and finally lead to death, then as soon as I am certain of this from the way things have gone, I will lovingly accept it in the highest part of my mind in spite of all opposition from my soul's lower powers. "Yes, Lord," I will say, "I truly desire this 'because such is Your good pleasure.'[184] Thus it has pleased You; thus also it pleases me, the most lowly minister of Your will."

But if God's good pleasure was declared to us before the actual event, as were the manner of his death to the great St. Peter,[185] chains and imprisonment to the great Paul,[186] the destruction of his beloved Jerusalem to Jeremiah,[187] and the death of his son to David,[188] then at that very instant, we must unite our will to God's will. We must follow the example of the great Abraham. Like him, if we are so commanded, we must undertake fulfillment of the eternal decree even by the death of our own children. Admirable was the union of that patriarch with God's will! Believing that it was the divine good pleasure for him to sacrifice his own child, he most courageously willed and undertook to do so! Admirable was the will

[184]Cf. Matt. 11:26.
[185]John 21:18-19.
[186]Acts 20:23; 21:11.
[187]Jer. 37:6-7.
[188]2 Kings 12:14 (RSV = 2 Sam. 12:14).

of the child who submitted so meekly to his father's sword so as to make God's good pleasure live even at the cost of his own death![189]

But take note, Theotimus, of what is characteristic of the perfect union of an indifferent heart with God's good pleasure. Behold Abraham with drawn sword, arm upraised, ready to give the death blow to his beloved, his only child. He does this to please the divine will. Behold at the same time an angel who at the behest of that same will stops him short. Immediately he checks his stroke, equally ready to sacrifice or not to sacrifice his son.[190] In the presence of God's will, the child's life and death were indifferent to him. When God commanded him to sacrifice the child, he did not become sad; when God dispensed him from it, he did not rejoice. It was all equal to that great heart, provided that God's will was served.

Yes, Theotimus, to train us in such holy indifference, God very often inspires us with most lofty plans, but does not will that they succeed. Then, just as we must confidently, courageously, and constantly begin and pursue the work as long as possible, so also we must humbly and calmly acquiesce in whatever outcome God is pleased to give to the enterprise.

By inspiration St. Louis went overseas to conquer the Holy Land; the outcome was contrary to his wish, and he humbly accepted it. I rate more highly that tranquil acceptance than the nobility of soul behind the project. St. Francis went to Egypt either to convert the infidels or to die a martyr among

[189]Gen. 22:1-12.
[190]Gen. 22:10-12.

the infidels.[191] Such was God's will. He came back without having done either the one or the other. Such too was God's will. It was equally God's will for St. Anthony of Padua to desire martyrdom and not to obtain it. When the Blessed Ignatius Loyola had put on foot the company of the name of Jesus,[192] he saw from it many fair fruits and foresaw many more in time to come. Nevertheless, he had the courage to resolve that even though he should see it all dissipated — which would be the bitterest sorrow he could receive — within half an hour afterward, he would be resolute and calm in God's will. That holy and learned preacher of Andalusia, John of Avila,[193] planned to form a company of priests dedicated to the advancement of God's glory and had already made great progress in his plan. As soon as he saw that the Jesuits were in the field, he thought that they were enough for that time, and with incomparable meekness and humility, brought his own project to an end.

How blessed are such souls, bold and strong in undertakings that God proposes to them and yet ready and humble to give them up when God so disposes! The following are marks of most perfect indifference: to leave off doing some good when to do so pleases God, and to return after going halfway when it is so ordained by God's will, which is our guide.

Jonah was greatly at fault in being downcast because God, as he thought, did not fulfill His prophecy for Nineveh.[194] Jonah

---

[191]St. Francis of Assisi and eleven companions made a preaching tour to Egypt in 1219.

[192]In other words, the Society of Jesus.

[193]St. John of Avila (1500-1569), Spanish mystic.

[194]Jon. 4:1-4.

did God's will in proclaiming the destruction of Nineveh, but he mingled his own interests and will with those of God. Hence when he saw that God did not fulfill His prediction in the strict sense of the words used in announcing it, Jonah was offended and murmured with indignation. If the good plea-sure of the divine will had been the sole motive of his actions, he would have been just as content in seeing it accomplished in the remission of the penalty Nineveh had merited as in seeing it satisfied by punishment of the fault Nineveh had committed.

We desire that what we undertake or manage shall suc-ceed, but it is unreasonable that God should do everything af-ter our liking. If God wills that Nineveh be threatened but not destroyed, since the threat is sufficient to correct it, why should Jonah complain?

If this is so, are we to care for nothing and abandon our af-fairs to the mercy of events? Not at all, Theotimus. We must forget nothing of whatever is requisite for bringing the work God has put in our hands to a successful conclusion. However, this is always on condition that if the outcome is contrary, we will lovingly and peacefully embrace it. We are commanded to have great care about things that pertain to God's glory and are in our charge, but we are not responsible for or charged with the outcome, since it is not in our power. "Take care of him," it was said to the innkeeper in the parable of the poor man who lay half-dead between Jerusalem and Jericho.[195] As St. Bernard remarks, it was not said, "Cure him," but, "Take care of him."[196]

---

[195] Luke 10:30-35.
[196] See St. Bernard, *De consideratione*, Bk. 4, ch. 2, n. 2.

So the apostles with matchless affection preached first to the Jews, although they knew that in the end they would be forced to leave them as unfruitful soil and to turn to the Gentiles.[197]

It is our part to plant and water carefully, but to give the increase belongs only to God.[198]

The great psalmist makes this prayer to the Savior, as if crying out in joy and as a presage of victory: "O Lord, with Your comeliness and Your beauty, bend Your bow, proceed prosperously, and mount Your horse."[199] It is as though he meant that by darts of His heavenly love shot into human hearts, He would make Himself the master of men so as to manage them according to His pleasure exactly like a well-trained horse.

> Lord, You are the royal cavalier who turns the hearts of Your faithful lovers about in every way. Sometimes You urge them forward with full rein, and they run at full speed in the tasks to which You inspire them. Then when it seems good to You, You make them stop in mid-career, and when strongest in their course.

Further, if a task undertaken by inspiration collapses by fault of those to whom it was committed, how can we say that a man must then acquiesce in God's will? Someone will say to me that it is not God's will that prevents success, but my own fault, of which the divine will is not the cause. It is true, my child, that your fault did not come about by God's will, for

---

[197] Acts 13:46-47.
[198] Cf. 1 Cor. 3:6-7.
[199] Cf. Ps. 44:5 (Septuagint; RSV = Ps. 45:4).

God is not the author of sin. Still for all that, it is God's will that your fault should be followed by the failure and collapse of your undertaking as a punishment of your fault. Although His goodness cannot permit Him to will your fault, yet His justice makes Him will the punishment you suffer for it. Thus God was not the cause of David's sin, but God truly inflicted upon him the punishment due to his sin.[200] God was not the cause of Saul's sin, but assuredly He was the cause that in punishment victory fell from Saul's hands.[201]

Therefore, when it happens that, in punishment of our faults, holy projects do not succeed, we must equally detest the fault by solid repentance and accept the punishment we have received for it. Just as the sin is against God's will, so also the punishment is according to His will.

[200] 2 Kings 12:9-14 (RSV = 2 Sam. 12:9-14).
[201] 1 Kings 31:1-4 (1 Sam. 31:1-4).

Do not be discouraged
by your failings

God has ordered us to do all we can to acquire holy virtues. Therefore, let us forget nothing that can bring success in this devout enterprise. But after we have planted and watered, we must realize that it is for God to give the increase[202] to the trees that are our good inclinations and habits. For this reason we must wait to obtain the fruits of our desires and labors from His Divine Providence. If we do not find our soul's progress and advance in the devout life to be such as we would like, let us not be disturbed, let us abide in peace, so that tranquillity may always reign in our hearts. It is for us to cultivate our souls well, and therefore we must faithfully attend to them. But as for plentiful crops and harvests, let us leave care of that to our Lord. The laborer will never be blamed for not having a fine harvest, unless he did not carefully till and sow his fields.

We should not be troubled at finding ourselves always novices in the exercise of virtue. In the monastery of the devout life, every man knows himself to be always a novice, and the whole of our life is destined to be a probation. There is no clearer proof that one is not only a novice, but worthy of expulsion and reprobation, than to think and hold oneself to be

[202]Cf. 1 Cor. 3:7.

professed. According to the rule of that order, it is not the solemn ceremony but the fulfillment of its vows that turns novices into professed members. Its vows are never fulfilled as long as anything remains to be done for their observance. The obligation of serving God and making progress in His love always lasts until death.

But after all, someone will say, if I know that it is by my own fault that my progress in virtue is delayed, how can I help being sad and disturbed? I have said this in the *Introduction to the Devout Life*,[203] but I gladly say it again because it can never be said often enough. For faults committed, we must have sorrow with repentance that is strong, settled, constant, and tranquil, but not turbulent, not unquiet, and not discouraged. Do you know that your slow progress on the road to virtue has come from your own fault? Well, then, humble yourself before God, implore His mercy, fall prostrate before the face of His goodness and ask His pardon, confess your fault, and cry to God for mercy in the very ear of your confessor so as to obtain absolution for it. This done, remain in peace. After you have detested the offense, lovingly embrace the abjection that is in you because of delaying your advance in good.

Ah, my Theotimus, beyond doubt souls in Purgatory are there because of their sins, sins that they have detested and that they supremely detest. But as for the abjection and pain that remain with them at being detained in that place, and at being temporarily deprived of enjoying the blessed love that is in Paradise, they suffer it lovingly, and devoutly utter the canticle of divine justice: "You are just, O Lord, and Your judgment

---

[203]*Introduction to the Devout Life*, Part 3, ch. 9.

is right."[204] Therefore, let us patiently wait for our advance, and instead of disturbing ourselves because we have made so little progress in the past, let us diligently strive to do better in the future.

༄

Transform temptations into
opportunities to grow in spiritual valor

Consider this good soul, I pray you. It has desired and tried hard to get rid of anger, and in this God has assisted it, for He has completely freed it from all sins that arise from anger. It would rather die than utter a single harmful word or let any sign of hatred slip out. Yet it is still subject to the attacks and first movements of this passion; that is, to certain impulses, movements, and outbursts of an irritated heart. The Chaldaic paraphrase calls them stirrings, and says, "Be stirred up and sin not," while our sacred version says, "Be angry and sin not."[205]

In effect it is the same thing. The prophet simply means that if anger catches us by surprise and excites in our hearts the first stirrings of anger, we should be most careful against letting ourselves be carried further into this passion so as to sin. Although these first movements and stirrings are not sins, yet the unfortunate soul that often is attacked by them becomes troubled, afflicted, and disturbed. It thinks that it does well in being sad, as if it were the love of God that provoked it to such sadness. Still, Theotimus, it is not heavenly love that causes this trouble, for it is never offended except by sin. It is our own

[204]Ps. 118:137 (RSV = Ps. 119:137).
[205]Ps. 4:5 (RSV = Ps. 4:4).

self-love that desires to be exempt from the pains and trials the attacks of anger bring on us. It is not the offense that displeases us in these stirrings of anger, since there is no sin whatsoever. It is the trouble of resisting them that disturbs us.

Such rebellions of the sensuous appetite, both in anger and in concupiscence, are left in us for our discipline to the end that we may exercise spiritual valor by resisting them. This is that Philistine whom the true Israelites must always fight against but can never subdue.[206] They can weaken but never destroy him. He never dies except when we die, and he always lives with us. He is truly accursed and detestable, since he issues from sin, and in practice, tends to sin. Wherefore, just as we are called earth, because we are taken from earth and shall return to earth,[207] so this rebellion is called sin by the great apostle as having come from sin and tending to sin, although it never makes us guilty unless we assent to it and obey it.[208]

Hence the apostle himself warns us not to permit this evil to reign in our mortal body so that we obey its lusts.[209] He does not forbid us to be aware of sin but only to consent to it. He does not order us to keep sin from coming into us and being in us, but he commands that it should not reign in us. It is in us when we perceive the rebellion of the sensual appetite, but it does not reign in us unless we give consent to it.

The physician never orders a man sick with fever not to be thirsty, as that would be a very foolish thing. He rightly tells

[206]Cf. Josh. 23:13.
[207]Gen. 3:19.
[208]Rom. 6-8.
[209]Rom. 6:12.

him that he must refrain from drinking even though he is thirsty. No one will tell a woman with child that she should not have a longing to eat strange things, for this is not in her power. She may well be told to tell what her appetite is, so that if it is for something harmful, they may divert her imagination and prevent such a fancy from reigning over her brain.

"A sting of the flesh, an angel of Satan,"[210] roughly attacked the great St. Paul in order to make him fall into sin. The poor apostle suffered this as a shameful and infamous wrong, and for this reason called it humiliation and buffeting and begged that God would deign to deliver him from it. God answered him, "Paul, my grace is sufficient for you, for strength is made perfect in infirmity." That great and holy man acquiesced in this and said, "Gladly will I glory in my infirmities, that the power of Christ may dwell in me."[211]

But please note well that there is sensual rebellion even in that admirable vessel of election.[212] When he runs to the remedy of prayer, he shows us that we must fight by those same means against the temptations we feel. Note further that if our Lord permits such cruel rebellions in man, it is not always to punish some sin, but to manifest the strength and power of divine assistance and grace.

Finally, note that we must not only not be disturbed amid temptations and infirmities but we must even glory in our infirmities so that God's power may appear in us, sustaining our weakness against the power of suggestion and temptation. The

[210]2 Cor. 12:7.
[211]Cf. 2 Cor. 12:8-9.
[212]Acts 9:15.

glorious apostle calls the stings and attacks of impurity that he felt his infirmities. He says that he glories in them, because although he feels them keenly by his misery, still by God's mercy he does not consent to them.

In fact, as I have already said, the Church condemned the error of certain solitaries who claimed that even in this world, we can be completely free from the passions of anger, lust, fear, and others like them.[213] God wills that we have certain enemies, and God wills that we should repulse them. Therefore, let us live courageously between these two aspects of God's will, suffering with patience when we are assailed and valiantly trying to make headway against our assailants and to resist them.

∾

Do not despair over the sins of others

God has supreme hatred for sin, and yet He most wisely permits it. This is to allow rational creatures to act according to their natural condition; it is also to render the good more worthy of commendation when they do not violate the law, even though they are able to violate it. Let us therefore adore and bless this holy permission.

However, since the same Providence that permits sin has infinite hatred for it, let us together with Providence detest and hate it, desiring with all our power that sin permitted may never become sin committed. As a result of this desire, let us use all possible remedies to prevent the birth, growth, and domination of sin. In this let us imitate our Lord, who never ceases to exhort, promise, threaten, prohibit, command, and

---

[213] See *Treatise on the Love of God*, Bk. 1, ch. 3.

inspire us in order to turn our will away from sin as far as possible without depriving it of liberty.

But when a sin has been committed, we must do all in our power to have it wiped away. We should be like our Lord, who assured Carpus, as has already been noted, that if it were needful, He would submit to death a second time in order to deliver a single soul from sin.[214] But if the sinner is obstinate, Theotimus, in company with the Savior of our souls, let us weep, sigh, and pray for him. For after He had shed many tears throughout His life over sinners and over those who represent them, He at last died, His eyes filled with tears, His body drenched in blood, lamenting the loss of sinners. Such affection touched David so keenly that he fell fainting before it. "A fainting has seized me because of the sinners who abandon Your law," he says.[215] And the great apostle protests that he has "a continuous sorrow"[216] in his heart because of the obstinacy of the Jews.

Meanwhile, no matter how obstinate sinners may be, we must never lose courage in aiding and serving them. How do we know whether perhaps they will do penance and be saved? Happy is he who, like St. Paul, can say to his neighbor, "Day and night I did not cease with tears to admonish every one of you. Therefore I am innocent of the blood of all, for I have not shrunk from declaring to you the whole counsel of God."[217] As long as we are within the limits of hope that the sinner can

---

[214]See page 15.
[215]Cf. Ps. 118:53 (RSV = Ps. 119:53).
[216]Cf. Rom. 9:2.
[217]Cf. Acts 20:31, 26, 27.

amend, and they are always of the same extent as those of his life, we must never reject him, but rather pray for him and help him as far as his misfortune will permit.

But at the very end, after we have wept over the obstinate and have rendered them our duty in charity of trying to reclaim them from perdition, we must imitate our Lord and the apostles. That is, we must turn our mind from them and place it on other objects and tasks more useful to God's glory. "It was necessary that the word of God should be first spoken to you," said the apostles to the Jews, "but since you reject it and judge yourselves unworthy" of the kingdom of Jesus Christ, "behold, we turn to the Gentiles."[218]

"The kingdom of God," says the Savior, "shall be taken from you and shall be given to a nation yielding its fruits."[219] We cannot spend too much time weeping over some men without losing time suitable and necessary to procure the salvation of others. True, the apostle says that he has "a continuous sorrow" over the loss of the Jews, but this is the same as when we say that we bless God at all times,[220] which means simply that we bless Him very frequently and on every occasion. In the same manner, the glorious St. Paul had a continuous sorrow in his heart because of the reprobation of the Jews, since on every occasion he lamented their misfortune.

For the rest, we must always adore, love, and praise God's avenging and punitive justice, just as we love His mercy, since both are daughters of His goodness. By His grace, He wills to

[218]Cf. Acts 13:46.
[219]Matt. 21:43.
[220]Ps. 33:1 (RSV = Ps. 34:1).

make us good, for He is good, yes, supremely good. By His justice, He wills to punish sin because He hates it, and He hates it because, being supremely good, He hates that supreme evil which is iniquity.

In conclusion, note that God never withdraws His mercy from us except by the most equitable vengeance of His punitive justice, and that we never escape the rigor of His justice except by His justifying mercy. Always, whether He punishes or gives grace, His good pleasure is worthy of adoration, love, and everlasting blessing. Hence "the just man" who sings the praises of God's mercy over such as shall be saved likewise "shall rejoice when he shall see vengeance."[221] With joy the blessed shall approve the judgment of damnation passed on the reprobate as well as that of salvation on the elect.

Since the angels have exercised their charity toward the men they had in their keeping, they shall remain in peace when they see them obstinate or even damned. Therefore, we must acquiesce in God's will and kiss the right hand of His mercy and the left hand of His justice with equal tenderness and reverence.

[221]Cf. Ps. 57:11 (RSV = Ps. 58:10).

Chapter Six

∽

Purify your love
for God

One of the world's finest musicians, who played the lute to perfection, in a brief time became so extremely deaf that he completely lost the use of hearing. However, in spite of that, he did not give up singing and playing the lute, doing so with marvelous delicacy by reason of his great skill, which his deafness had not taken away. He had no pleasure either in singing or in the sound of the lute, since after his loss of hearing, he could not perceive their sweetness and beauty. Hence he no longer sang or played except to entertain a prince whose native subject he was and whom he had a great inclination, as well as an infinite obligation, to please, since he had been brought up from his youth in the prince's court. For this reason he had the very greatest pleasure in pleasing the prince, and he was overjoyed when the prince showed that he enjoyed his music.

Sometimes it happened that, to test this loving musician's love, the prince would command him to sing and immediately leave him there in the room and go out hunting. The singer's desire to fulfill his master's wishes made him continue his song just as attentively as if the prince were present, although in fact he himself took no pleasure in singing. He had neither pleasure in the melody, for his deafness deprived him of that, nor that of pleasing the prince, since the prince was absent and hence could not enjoy the beautiful sweetness of the airs he sang.

> *My heart is ready, Lord, and all disposed*
> *To sound a song for Your high name composed.*
> *My heart and will and tongue will now upraise*
> *A song unto Your praise.*
> *Up, up, O glory mine, we must arise!*
> *Psalter and harp, unveil your sleeping eyes![222]*

∞

Strive to love God purely to please Him

The human heart is the true singer of the canticle of sacred love; it is itself both harp and psaltery. Ordinarily, this singer hears himself and takes great pleasure in listening to his melodious song. That is, when our heart loves God, it savors the delights of this love and takes incomparable contentment in loving an object so worthy of love.

I beg of you, Theotimus, to note what I mean. At first, small, young nightingales try to sing so as to imitate the large ones. But having been trained and become masters, they sing because of the pleasure they take in warbling. They become so passionately attached to this pleasure, as I have said elsewhere, that by force of straining their voices, their throats burst open and they die.[223]

So, too, at the beginning of their devotion, our hearts love God so as to be united to Him, to become agreeable to Him,

[222]Cf. Ps. 56:8-10 (RSV = Ps. 57:7-9).
[223]See *Treatise on the Love of God*, Bk. 5, ch. 8.

and to imitate Him, because He has eternally loved us. But little by little, after they are formed and trained in holy love, they imperceptibly bring about a change. In place of loving God in order to please God, they begin to love Him for the pleasure they themselves take in the exercises of holy love. Instead of being in love with God, they fall in love with the love they have for Him. They are attached to their own attachments. They no longer take pleasure in God, but in the pleasure they have in His love. They are content with this love because it is their own, because it is in their spirit, and because it proceeds from it.

Although this sacred love is called love of God because God is loved by it, yet it is ours also because by it we are lovers who love by its means. This is the reason for the change. Instead of loving this holy love because it tends to God, who is the beloved, we love it because it proceeds from us, who are the lovers. Who fails to see that in so doing, it is no longer God whom we seek, but that we return to ourselves? We love the love instead of loving the beloved. I say that we love this love not for God's good pleasure and contentment, but for the pleasure and contentment we ourselves take in it.

The singer, then, who in the beginning sang to God and for God now sings to himself and for himself rather than for God. If he takes pleasure in singing, it is not so much to delight God's ear as his own. Because the canticle of divine love is the most excellent of all songs, he also loves it better, not by reason of the divine excellence which is praised by it, but because the melody of such chanting is more delightful and agreeable.

You can easily recognize this, Theotimus: if this mystic nightingale sings to please God, it will sing the canticle it knows to be most agreeable to Divine Providence. However, if it sings for the pleasure it takes in its own melodious singing, it will not sing the canticle most pleasing to heavenly goodness, but that which is most pleasing to its own taste, and from which it expects to draw most pleasure. Of two canticles, both of which are truly divine, it may well be that one will be sung because it is divine and the other because it is pleasant. Rachel and Leah are equally wives of Jacob, but the second is loved by him solely in her character as wife, while the first is loved in her character as a beautiful woman. The canticle is divine, but the motive that causes us to sing it is the spiritual delight we look for in it.

We may say to a certain bishop, "Do you not see that God wills you to sing the pastoral song of His love among your flock which, in the person of the great St. Peter, the first of pastors, he thrice commands you to feed?[224] What is your answer? That at Rome or Paris there are greater spiritual delights and that there we can practice divine love with more pleasure?" O God, it is not to please You that this man desires to sing, but for the pleasure he takes from his own song. It is not You whom he seeks in love but the contentment found in practices of holy love.

Men in religious orders would like to sing the pastors' song, and married men that of the religious, so that — they say this — they can love and serve God better. Oh, you deceive yourselves, my dear friends! Do not say that it is to love and serve God better! Oh, no indeed! It is to serve your own self-satisfaction better, for you love it more than God's contentment!

[224]John 21:15-17.

God's will is found in sickness as well as in health, ordinarily even more so. Therefore, if we love health better, let us not say that this is to serve God so much better. Who does not see that it is health that we seek for in God's will, and not God's will in health?

∞

Learn to distinguish between
love of God and self-love

It is not easy, I admit, to look with pleasure at the beauty of a mirror for a long time without looking at oneself in it; yes, without taking pleasure in looking at oneself. Still, there is a difference between the pleasure a man takes in looking at himself in a mirror because it is a fine one and the complacence he takes in looking at a mirror simply because he sees himself in it. Undoubtedly, it is also hard to love God without loving to some extent the pleasure we take in His love. However, there is a great difference between the satisfaction we take in loving God because of His beauty and that which we take in loving Him because His love is pleasing to us. We must strive to seek in God only love of His beauty and not the pleasure found in the beauty of His love.

If a man prays to God and perceives that he is praying, he is not perfectly attentive to his prayer. He diverts his attention from God, to whom he prays, in order to think of the prayer by which he prays. Our very care not to have distractions often serves as a very great distraction. In spiritual actions simplicity is most recommendable. Do you wish to contemplate God? Then turn your gaze on Him, and be attentive to that. If you reflect and turn your eyes down upon yourself to see how you look when you look at Him, then it is not God that you behold; it is your own behavior, it is yourself.

A man in fervent prayer does not know whether he prays or not, for he does not think of the prayer he makes, but of God, to whom he makes it. A man in the ardor of sacred love does not turn his heart back on himself to see what he is doing, but keeps it fixed on God and taken up with God, to whom he applies his love. The heavenly singer takes such pleasure in pleasing God that he takes no pleasure in his melodious voice unless it is because it pleases God.

Theotimus, why do you think that Amnon, David's son, loved Tamar so desperately that he even thought that he would die of love?[225] Do you think that it was Tamar herself whom he loved? You see very quickly that it was not, for as soon as he had satisfied his detestable desire, he ruthlessly drove her out and ignominiously cast her away.[226] If he had loved Tamar, he would not have done this. Tamar was always Tamar. But because it was not Tamar that he loved, but the vile pleasure that he looked for in her, as soon as he had what he wanted, he struck her viciously and treated her in a brutal way. His pleasure was in Tamar, but his love was for the pleasure and not for Tamar. Thus once his pleasure had gone, he willingly made Tamar go away.

Look at this man, Theotimus, who apparently prays to God with such devotion and is so ardent in the practice of heavenly love. Wait a little while, and you will see if it is God whom he loves. Unfortunately, as soon as the delight and satisfaction he took in love leaves him and dryness comes, he will give up all

[225] 2 Kings 13:2 (RSV = 2 Sam. 13:2).
[226] 2 Kings 13:14-17 (RSV = 2 Sam. 13:14-17).

that and he will say further prayers only at random. If it was God whom he loved, why did he cease to love, since God is always God? It was God's consolations that he loved, and not "the God of consolation."[227]

Many men indeed take no delight in divine love unless it is candied over with the sugar of some sensible sweetness. They would willingly act like little children who, when someone gives them a piece of bread with honey on it, lick and suck out the honey and then throw away the bread. If the sweetness could be separated from the love, such men would leave the love and take only the sweetness. The reason is that they follow love for the sake of sweetness, and when they do not find it, they hold love to be of no account. Such people are exposed to very great danger either of turning back when savors and consolations fail them, or else of beguiling themselves with vain delights far removed from true love.

∞

Love God even in the absence of consolations
After the musician of whom I have spoken became deaf, he had no pleasure in singing except sometimes in seeing his prince listen attentively to it and take pleasure in it. Happy is the heart that loves God with no other pleasure but that which it takes in pleasing God! What purer and more perfect pleasure can we ever have than that which we take in God's pleasure? Yet strictly speaking, this pleasure in pleasing God is not divine love, but only its fruit, which can be separated from it like citron from the citron tree. As I have said, our musician

[227]Cf. 2 Cor. 1:3.

always sang without taking any pleasure in his singing, since his deafness prevented it. Moreover, he often sang without having even the pleasure of pleasing the prince, for after having ordered him to sing, the prince would retire or go out hunting, taking neither the leisure to hear him nor the pleasure of hearing him.

> O God, as long as I see Your sweet face, which testifies to me that You are pleased with the song raised by my love, ah, how consoled am I! Is any pleasure equal to the pleasure of truly pleasing our God? But when You turn Your eyes away from me and I no longer perceive the sweet favor of Your complacence in my song, then, O true God, in what great torment is my soul! But still it does not cease to love You faithfully and to sing continually its hymn of love — not for any pleasure that it finds therein, for it has none at all — but for the pure love of Your holy will.

We have seen a sick child eating bravely but with incredible distaste what his mother gives him, solely out of desire to please her. He eats without taking any pleasure in the food, but not without another higher and worthier pleasure — namely, the pleasure of pleasing his mother and seeing her relief. Another child does not see his mother and solely for the knowledge he has of her wishes accepts whatever she sends and eats it without any pleasure. He has neither the pleasure of eating nor the satisfaction of seeing his mother's pleasure; he eats purely and simply to do her will.

Purify your love for God

The mere comfort of a prince's presence or that of someone we greatly love makes watching, pain, and toil a delight, and danger itself desirable. But nothing is so grievous as to serve a master who knows nothing of our service, or if he knows about it, still gives no sign that he is satisfied with it. In such cases, love must be strong, because it stands by itself alone, unsupported by any pleasure or any expectation. Thus it sometimes happens that we have no consolation in the exercises of sacred love, because like deaf singers, we do not hear our own voices and cannot enjoy the sweet melody of our song. Besides this we are oppressed by a thousand fears and troubled by a thousand false alarms that the enemy raises around our heart, suggesting to us that perhaps we are not pleasing to our master and that our love is fruitless — yes, even that it is false and vain, since it produces no consolation. Then, Theotimus, we toil not only without pleasure, but with very great distress, since we see neither the good of our labor nor the satisfaction of Him for whom we labor.

What increases the pain in this condition is that not even the spirit and the highest part of reason can afford us any kind of relief. Since this poor superior portion of our reason is completely surrounded by suggestions put to it by the enemy, it is itself filled with alarm, and is wholly engaged in keeping on guard, lest it be taken by surprise by some consent to evil. Therefore it cannot sortie forth to relieve the lower part of the spirit. Although it has not lost courage, it is under such terrible attack that it is not free from pain even though free from fault. To complete its distress, it is deprived of the general consolation we usually have among all other evils in this world; namely, the hope that they will not last long and that we will see their end.

Hence in such spiritual distress, the heart falls into a kind of impotence in thinking of its end and consequently of being relieved by hope. It is true that faith, which resides at the summit of the spirit, assures us that this trouble will have an end and that we shall enjoy a day of true rest. However, the great uproar and shouting that the enemy makes in the rest of the soul — namely, in the inferior reason — hardly allows the advice and remonstrances of faith to be heard. There remains in the imagination only this sorrowful foreboding: "Alas, I shall never find joy."[228]

It is now, my dear Theotimus, that we must show unconquerable fidelity to the Savior, serving Him purely for love of His will, not only without pleasure, but under this deluge of sorrow, horror, dread, and attack, as did His glorious Mother and St. John on the day of His Passion. Amid all the blasphemy, sorrow, and deadly distress, they remained firm in love — yes, even when the Savior, having withdrawn all His holy joy up into the very summit of His spirit, showed forth no joy or consolation at all on His divine face but, with eyes fading, and covered over with the shadows of death, cast down only looks of sorrow even as the sun cast down rays of horror and fearsome shadows.[229]

∞

When troubles assail you, trust in God
On the night before the great St. Peter was to be martyred, an angel came into his prison and filled it with splendor, awoke

[228]See *Introduction to the Devout Life*, Part 4, ch. 15.
[229]Cf. Luke 23:44-45.

St. Peter, made him arise, gird himself, and put on his sandals and clothing. Then he freed Peter from his bonds and shackles, took him out of prison, and led him "through the first and second guard until he came to the iron gate that leads into the city, which opened itself before them . . . and having passed through one street" the angel left the glorious St. Peter there in full freedom.[230]

In all this, there is a great variety of acts apparent to the senses; yet St. Peter, who was awake from the beginning, "did not know that what was done by the angel was real, but thought that it was a vision"[231] of his imagination. He was awake, but he did not think he was awake. He put on his sandals and clothes without knowing that he did so; he walked, but he did not know that he was walking; he was set free, but he did not believe it. This was because the marvelous character of his deliverance was so great as to fill his mind in such a way that while he had sense and knowledge sufficient to do what he did, he still did not have enough to recognize that he was really doing it in good earnest. He actually saw the angel, but he did not perceive that he saw him with true, natural vision. For this reason he had no consolation from his deliverance until he came to himself. "Now," he said, "I know for certain that the Lord has sent His angel, and has rescued me from the hand of Herod and from all that the Jewish people were expecting."[232]

It is the same way, Theotimus, with a soul that is heavily burdened with interior troubles. Although it has the power to

[230]Cf. Acts 12:6-10.
[231]Cf. Acts 12:9.
[232]Cf. Acts 12:11.

believe, hope in, and love God — and in fact does so — yet it does not have the strength to see clearly whether it believes, hopes in, and loves God. Its distress has such a hold on it and weighs so heavily upon it that it cannot turn back upon itself to see what it does. Hence it thinks that it has no faith, no hope, and no love, but only phantoms and useless impressions of those virtues. It knows them almost without knowing them, and as if they were strangers and not members of its own household.

If you will examine the matter, you will find that our minds are always in this same state when strongly seized by some violent passion. They do many things as if in a dream and are so little aware of them that they hardly know that the deeds have actually taken place. Hence the sacred psalmist expresses in these words the great consolation the Israelites felt on their return from captivity in Babylon:

> *When once by Babylon's fell stream*
> *God set his children free,*
> *Our joy seemed an enraptured dream,*
> *Too great, too fair to be!*[233]

As the holy Latin version, which follows the Septuagint, has it: "We became like men comforted." That is, our wonder at the great good that came to us was so excessive that it kept us from feeling properly the consolation we received. It seemed to us that we were not truly comforted, and did not have true consolation, but only an image and dream of it.

Such are the feelings of a soul that is sunk in spiritual anguish, which renders love exceedingly pure and clean. Being

[233]Cf. Ps. 125:1 (RSV = Ps. 126:1).

deprived of all pleasure by which it can be attached to God, such love joins and unites us immediately to God, will to will, heart to heart, without any intervening comfort or further expectation.

Alas, Theotimus, how afflicted our poor heart is when it is abandoned, as it were, by love, looks everywhere for it, and seems to find it nowhere. It does not find it in the external senses, for they are incapable of it; nor in the imagination, which is cruelly tormented by diverse impressions; nor in reason, which is troubled by a thousand obscure arguments and strange fears. Although it at last finds love in the very summit and supreme region of the spirit, where this divine love resides, yet the soul does not recognize it and thinks that it is not love, because its great distress and darkness hinder it from sensing its sweetness. It sees it without seeing it, encounters it without recognizing it, as if it were in a dream and in imagination. Thus when Magdalene encountered her dear Master, she received no comfort from Him because she thought that it was not He but only the gardener.[234]

What is a soul in this state to do? Theotimus, it does not know how to conduct itself in such great anguish. It has no further power except to let its will die in the hands of God's will in imitation of its own beloved Jesus. When He had come to the climax of those pains upon the Cross which His Father had ordained for Him, unable to resist further the extremity of His torments, He did as does the hart. When the hart has lost all breath and is beset by the hounds, gasping out its last sighs and with eyes filled with tears, it throws itself before the

[234]John 20:15.

huntsman. So when our divine Savior was near death and sending forth His last breath, with a loud cry and many tears He said, "Alas, O my Father, into Your hands I commend my spirit." [235] This was last of all His words, Theotimus, and by it, the beloved Son gave supreme testimony to His love for His Father.

Therefore, when all things fail us; when our distress is at its height, this word, this sentiment, this renunciation of our soul into the hands of our Savior cannot fail us. The Son commended His spirit to His Father in that last, incomparable anguish. And we, when convulsive spiritual torments deprive us of every other kind of relief and means of resistance, let us commend our spirit into the hands of the eternal Son, and "bowing the head"[236] of our acquiescence in His good pleasure, let us consign our entire will to Him.

[235] Cf. Luke 23:46.
[236] Cf. John 19:30.

Chapter Seven

∽∾

Abandon yourself completely
to God's will

～

In the French language, we speak with very special propriety
of men's death, for we call it a passing over, and we call the
dead those who have passed over. We thus signify that for men,
death is only a passage from one life to another and that to die
is simply to pass over the boundaries of this mortal life in order
to go into immortal life. Our will in fact can never die, no more
than our soul can, yet sometimes it passes over the boundaries
of its accustomed life so as to live wholly in the divine will. At
such times, it neither can nor wishes to will anything further,
but abandons itself entirely and without reserve to the good
pleasure of Divine Providence, so mingling and dissolving itself in this good pleasure that it no longer shows forth. It is
completely "hidden with Jesus Christ in God,"[237] where it is no
longer itself that lives but God's will that lives in it.[238]

What becomes of the light of the stars when the sun appears on the horizon? Such light does not actually perish, but
it is ravished and absorbed into the sun's supreme light with
which it is happily intermingled and joined. What becomes
of man's will when it is entirely abandoned to the divine good

[237]Cf. Col. 3:3.
[238]Cf. Gal. 2:20.

pleasure? It does not wholly perish, yet it is so engulfed in and intermingled with God's will that it no longer shows forth and has no further desire apart from God's will.

∞

Let yourself be led completely by God's will

Theotimus, picture the glorious and never sufficiently praised St. Louis as he embarks and sets sail to travel overseas. See, too, the queen, his dear wife, as she embarks with his majesty. Now, if anyone had asked that valiant princess, "Madam, where are you going?" she would doubtless have replied, "I am going where the king is going." If asked further, "But, madam, do you really know where the king is going?" she would have answered thus: "He told me in general. However, I do not care to know where he is going. I only want to go with him." And if someone had replied, "But, madam, have you no purpose in this journey?" "No," she would have said, "I have none except to be with my dear lord and husband." "But in fact," it might have been said to her, "he is going to Egypt in order to proceed on into Palestine. He will stay at Damietta, Acre, and many other places. Do you not intend, madam, to go there also?"

To this she would have answered: "No, truly, I have no intention except only to be with my king. The places to which he is going are all a matter of indifference and of no concern to me except that he will be there. I am going with no desire to go, for I am concerned with nothing except the king's presence. Therefore, it is the king who is going and desires the journey. As for me, I do not go; I only follow. I do not desire this journey, but solely the king's presence. Sojourn, journey, and every kind of change are completely indifferent to me."

Abandon yourself to God's will

If we ask some servant in his master's retinue where he is going, he would not answer that he is going to such and such a place but simply that he accompanies his master, since he goes nowhere of his own will, but only at his master's will. In like manner, Theotimus, a will perfectly resigned to God's will should have no other will but simply to follow God's will. Just as a man on board ship does not move by his own proper motion, but lets himself be moved solely by the motion of the vessel in which he is, in like manner, the heart that is embarked in the divine good pleasure should have no other will but that of permitting itself to be led by God's will. In such case, the heart no longer says, "Your will be done, not mine,"[239] for there is now no will to renounce. It says these words, "Lord, into Your hands I commend my will,"[240] as though it did not have its will at its own disposal but only at that of Divine Providence.

Therefore, it is not exactly the same as with servants who accompany their masters. Even if the journey is undertaken at their master's will, still their attendance on him is made by their own individual will, although it is a will that follows and serves and submits and is subjected to that of their master. Hence just as master and servant are two persons, so also the master's will and that of the servant are two wills. But the will that is dead to itself so as to live in God's will is without any particular desire, and remains not only in conformity and subjection, but is totally annihilated in itself and is converted into God's will.

[239]Cf. Luke 22:42.
[240]Cf. Ps. 30:6 (RSV = Ps. 31:5); Luke 23:46.

Finding God's Will for You

It is like what might be said of a little child who does not yet have use of his will so as to desire or love anything except his dear mother's breast and face. He does not think of wanting to be on one side or the other, or of desiring anything else whatever save only to be in the arms of his mother, with whom he thinks himself to be one being. He is never at pains to adapt his will to his mother's, for he does not know his own will and does not think he has one. To his mother he leaves complete care to go, to do, and to will what she finds good for him.

Assuredly, our will's supreme perfection is to be thus united to that of our Supreme Good, as was the will of that saint who said, "O Lord, You have conducted me and led me by Your will."[241] What does he mean unless it is that he has not used his own will to conduct himself, but has let himself simply be guided and led by that of his God?

∞

Strive to will nothing for yourself
but what God wills for you

We may rightly believe that the most holy Virgin, our Lady, took such joy in carrying her beloved Child Jesus in her arms that it kept her from growing weary, or at least made such weariness pleasant to her. If a branch of *agnus castus* can comfort travelers and ease their weariness, what relief must the glorious Mother have received when she carried "the immaculate Lamb of God!"[242] Although she sometimes permitted Him to walk with her on His own feet while she held Him by the hand,

[241]Cf. Ps. 72:24 (RSV = Ps. 73:23-24).
[242]Cf. John 1:36; 1 Pet. 1:19.

128

this was not because she did not prefer to have Him cling to her neck and on her breast, but to teach Him how to place His steps and to walk alone.

We ourselves, Theotimus, as little children of our heavenly Father, can walk with Him in two ways. In the first way, we can walk with the steps of our own will, which we conform to His, holding always with the hand of our obedience the hand of His divine intention and following wherever it leads us. This is what God requires of us by His will as signified to us. Since He wills that I do what He ordains, He wills me to have the will to do it. God has signified that He wills me to keep holy the day of rest. Since He wills that I do this, He then wills that I will to do it, and that for this end I have a will of my own by which I follow His by conforming and corresponding to it.

But we can also walk with our Lord without having any will of our own. We simply let ourselves be carried by His divine good pleasure, just as a little child is carried in his mother's arms, by a certain kind of admirable consent that may be called the union, or rather the unity, of our will with that of God. This is the way in which we should strive to let ourselves be borne forward in the will of God's good pleasure. The effects of this will of good pleasure proceed purely from His Providence. We do not make them, but they befall us. It is true that we can will them to come in accordance with God's will, and this will is most good. Yet we can also receive the outcome of Heaven's good pleasure with a most unalloyed tranquillity of will that wills nothing whatsoever, but acquiesces absolutely in all that God wills to be done in us, on us, or by us.

If someone had asked the beloved Child Jesus, when He was being carried in His Mother's arms, where He was going,

He might have justly replied, "I am not going; it is my Mother who goes for me." If He had then been asked, "But do you not at least go with your Mother?" He might have reasonably replied, "No, I do not go at all, or if I go where my Mother carries me, I do not go along with her or by means of my own steps, but I go only by my Mother's steps, by her and on her." But if someone replied to Him, "But, most divine Child, at least you really will to let yourself be carried by your own sweet Mother," "No indeed," He might have said, "I do not do so. I will nothing of all that. But just as my best of Mothers walks for me, so also she wills for me. I leave to her equally the care both to go and to will to go in my behalf wherever she likes best. Just as I walk only by means of her steps, so also I will only by means of her will. From the moment I find myself in her arms, I do not have thought either of willing or of not willing. I leave all other care to my Mother, save only the care to be on her bosom, to feed at her sacred breast, and to keep myself clasped to her dearest neck so that I may most lovingly kiss her 'with the kisses of my mouth.'[243]

"That you may know that while I am in the midst of the delights of these holy caresses, which surpass all sweetness, I reflect that my Mother is a tree of life and that I am with her as its fruit, that I am her own heart within her breast, or her soul within her heart. For this reason, just as when she walks, it suffices both for her and for me — without exertion of any sort on my part — so also her will suffices both for her and for me without my making any volition either to go or to come. Again, I do not notice if she walks quickly or very softly, or if

[243] Cf. Cant. 1:1 (RSV = Song of Sol. 1:2).

she goes to one place or to another. I do not ask where she means to go, but am satisfied that wherever it may be I am always within her arms, joined to her loving breast where I am fed as 'among the lilies.' "[244]

> O divine Child of Mary, grant my poor soul
> to send forth this outburst of love! Go then, O
> little Child most lovable and most cherished; or
> rather, go not but stay thus piously fastened
> to the breast of Your own sweet Mother! Go
> always on her and by her or with her, and never
> go without her as long as You are a child. O
> how "blessed is the womb that bore You and
> the breasts that gave You suck!"[245]

Theotimus, we must be like that, always rendering ourselves pliable and tractable to God's good pleasure, as though we were wax. We must not trick ourselves into willing and wishing for things, but leave them to God for Him to will and do them for us as He pleases, "casting all our anxiety upon Him, because He cares for us,"[246] as the holy apostle says. Note that he says, "all our anxiety," that is, not only our anxiety as to accepting events but also that of willing or not willing them. He will have care as to the outcome of our affairs and to will whatever is best for us.

Meanwhile, let us lovingly use our care to bless God in all that He does, saying after the example of Job, "The Lord has

[244]Cant. 2:16 (RSV = Song of Sol. 2:16).
[245]Luke 11:27.
[246]Cf. 1 Pet. 5:7.

given much to me, and the Lord has taken it away from me. Blessed be the name of the Lord."[247]

> *No, Lord, I do not will any event. I leave events to You to will them for me entirely as You please. Instead of willing events, I will bless You because You have willed them.*

Oh, how excellent, Theotimus, is this use of our will, when it gives up all care to will and choose the effects of God's good pleasure in order to praise and thank that good pleasure for such effects!

∞

Seek perfection in submission to God's will

To bless God and to thank Him for whatever events His Providence ordains is truly a most holy exercise. However, while we leave to God the care of willing and doing in us, on us, and with us whatever pleases Him, without attending to what occurs — even though we feel it fully — then, if we can divert our hearts and fix our attention on God's goodness and sweetness, blessing it not in its effects and in the events it ordains, but in itself and in its own perfection, we will undoubtedly perform a still higher exercise.

When Demetrius laid siege to Rhodes, Protogenes,[248] who was in a little house in the outskirts, never stopped working with complete assurance and peace of mind. Although a sword was always at his throat, he produced his greatest masterpiece,

[247]Cf. Job 1:21.
[248]Protogenes, fourth-century Greek painter.

a marvelous satyr playing upon a pipe.[249] How great are those souls who, amid vicissitudes of every kind, always keep their thoughts and affections fastened on eternal goodness so as to honor and cherish it forever.

The daughter of a very able physician and surgeon, who knew that her father loved her perfectly, lay in a continual fever and said to one of her friends: "I feel a great deal of pain, but I never think about any remedies, for I do not know what could bring about a cure. I might desire one thing, whereas another would be needed. Do I not gain more by leaving all this in my father's care, since he has the knowledge, the ability, and the will to do for me whatever is necessary for my health? I would be wrong to give any thought to such things, since he will think of enough things for me. I would be wrong to want anything, for he will determine in sufficient measure all that will help me. I will only wait until he wills to do whatever he judges expedient. When he is with me, I will be content to look at him, show him my filial love, and make known my perfect confidence in him."

After these words she fell asleep, while her father, who had decided that it was necessary to bleed her, arranged whatever was required. He then came to awaken her, questioned her as to how she had slept, and asked her if she was willing to be bled as a cure. "Father," she said, "I am yours. I do not know what cure to wish for myself. It is for you to will and do for me whatever seems good to you. As for me, it is enough for me to love and honor you with all my heart, as I do." Hence her arm was tied and her father himself applied the lancet to the vein.

[249]Cf. Pliny the Elder, *Natural History*, Bk. 35, ch. 36.

While he made the incision and the blood flowed forth, his loving daughter never looked at her pierced arm or at the blood spurting from the vein, but kept her eyes fixed on her father's face. From time to time she softly said only this: "My father loves me dearly, and I am wholly his." When all this was finished, she did not thank him but only repeated once more those same words of filial affection and confidence.

Tell me now, Theotimus, my friend, did not this daughter show a more thoughtful and solid love for her father than if she had been very careful to ask him about remedies for her malady, watch him as he opened the vein and the blood flowed out, and say many words of thanks to him? There is no doubt whatever about it. If she had been thinking about herself, what would she have gained except unneeded care, since her father had care enough for her? What would she have gained from looking at her arm except fear? By thanking her father, what virtue but gratitude would she have practiced? Was it not better for her to concern herself entirely with the demonstration of her filial love, which was infinitely more pleasing to her father than every other virtue?

"My eyes are always toward the Lord, for He will free my feet from the snare"[249] and from the nets. Have you fallen into the snare of adversity? Ah, do not look at your mishap or at the snare in which you are caught. Look upon God and leave everything to Him, for He will take care of you. "Cast your care upon the Lord, and He will support you."[250] Why do you disturb yourself with willing or not willing the events and

[249]Cf. Ps. 24:15 (RSV = Ps. 25:15).
[250]Cf. Ps. 54:23 (RSV = Ps. 55:22); 1 Pet. 5:7.

accidents of this world? You do not know what you ought to will, and God will always will in sufficient measure all you could will for yourself without putting yourself in trouble.

Therefore, wait in peace of mind for the effects of God's good pleasure. Let His willing always be sufficient for you, since it is always the best. Thus it was that He ordered His beloved St. Catherine of Siena, for He said to her, "Think in me, and I will think for you."[251]

It is very difficult to put into exact words this highest indifference of the human will, which is thus reduced to God's will and has perished in it. It seems to me that we must not say that it acquiesces in God's will, since acquiescence is an act of the soul declaring its assent. We must not say that it accepts or receives, because to accept and to receive are actions that to a certain extent might be called "passive actions" by which we embrace and take what happens to us. Nor must we say that it permits, since permission is an act of the will, and hence a kind of inert willing. It does not actually will to do a thing, but still it wills to let it be done.

Rather, it seems to me that the soul that is in this state of indifference and wills nothing, but leaves it to God to will what is pleasing to Him, must be said to have its will in a simple and general state of waiting. To wait is neither to do nor to act, but only to remain subject to some event. If you will examine the matter, this waiting on the part of the soul is truly voluntary.

Nevertheless, it is not an action but rather a simple disposition to receive whatever shall happen. As soon as the events

---

[251]Cf. Blessed Raymond of Capua, *Vita s. Catherinae sensensis*, Part 1, ch. 9.

take place and are received, the waiting changes into consent or acquiescence. But before they occur, the soul is truly in a state of simple waiting, indifferent to all that the divine will is pleased to ordain.

Our Savior thus expresses the total submission of His human will to the will of His eternal Father. "The Lord God has opened my ear," He says.[252] That is, "He has declared to me His good pleasure regarding the many sufferings I must endure." He continues and says, "I do not resist. I have not gone back."[253] What does He mean by these statements — "I do not resist. I have not gone back" — except the following? "My will is in a state of simple waiting; it remains ready for all that God will ordain. Therefore 'I have given' and abandoned 'my body to the strikers, and my cheeks to them that plucked them.'[254] I was prepared for all they wished to do to me."

But, I pray you, Theotimus, see how it was with our Savior after He had made His prayer of resignation in the Garden of Olives and had been seized.[255] Just as He let Himself be pulled and dragged about at the will of them who crucified Him — with wonderful abandonment of His body and life to their hands — so also with most perfect indifference, He placed His soul and will in the hands of His eternal Father. Although he cried out, "My God, my God, why have You forsaken me?"[256] this was to make known to us how real were His bitterness and

[252]Isa. 50:5.
[253]Ibid.
[254]Isa. 50:6.
[255]Matt. 26:39-50.
[256]Matt. 27:46.

torment of soul, and not to violate the most holy indifference in which He was. He showed this very soon afterward as He concluded His whole life and His Passion with these incomparable words. "Father, into Your hands I commend my spirit."[257]

༄

Love God's will above all else

Let us represent to ourselves, Theotimus, Jesus standing submissively in Pilate's house, where for love of us He was stripped of all His garments, one after the other, by soldiers, the ministers of His death. Not satisfied with this, they took His very skin from him, tearing it off by blows of their staves and whips. Later, His soul was in like manner stripped of its body and His body of its life by the death He endured upon the Cross. But after three days had passed, by His most holy Resurrection, His soul put on again His glorious body, and His body, its immortal skin. Then, too, He clothed Himself in various garments; now those of a gardener or a pilgrim, or of some other kind, according as the salvation of men and the glory of God required.

Love did all this, Theotimus. It is love also that, entering a soul to make it happily die to itself and live again in God, strips it of all human desires and self-esteem, which is as closely fixed to our spirit as skin to flesh. At length it denudes that soul of its dearest affections, such as those it had for spiritual consolations, devout exercises, and perfect virtue, which seemed to be the very life of a devout soul.

At such times, Theotimus, the soul is right to cry out, "I have put off my garments: shall I put them on again? I have

[257]Luke 23:46.

washed my feet of affections of every kind: shall I defile them again?[258] Naked I came forth from the hand of God, and naked I shall go back again. The Lord gave me many desires, the Lord has taken them away; blessed be His holy name."[259] Yes, Theotimus, the same Lord who makes us desire those virtues at the beginning of our course and makes us practice them amid all eventualities is He who takes away affection for virtues and all spiritual exercises to the end that, with tranquillity, purity, and simplicity, we may have affection for nothing but the good pleasure of His divine majesty.

Judith, the beautiful and chaste, kept her costly festive robes stored away in a closet, but had no liking for them and never wore them during her widowhood except at the time when, by God's inspiration, she went out to destroy Holofernes.[260] In like manner, although we have learned virtuous practices and devout exercises, we must have no affection for them, nor reclothe our hearts with them except only insofar as we know that such is God's good pleasure. Just as Judith always wore mourning garments except on that occasion when God willed that she be dressed with pomp, so also we must remain peaceably clothed with misery and abjection amid our imperfections and infirmities until God raises us up to the practice of excellent actions.

We cannot long remain in such nakedness, stripped of every kind of affection. Hence, according to the advice of the holy apostle, after we have put off the garments of the old Adam, we must put on the clothing of the new man; that is, of Jesus

---

[258]Cf. Cant. 5:3 (RSV = Song of Sol. 5:3).
[259]Cf. Job 1:21.
[260]Jth. 10:3.

Christic.[261] Having renounced all things — yes, even affection for virtue — so as to desire among them and all other things only what God's good pleasure will grant, we must clothe ourselves anew with various affections, perhaps with the very ones we have renounced and given up. But we must put them on again, no longer because they are agreeable, profitable, and honorable to us, and suited to satisfy our self-love, but because they are agreeable to God, profitable to His honor, and destined for His glory.

Eliezer carried earrings, bracelets, and new garments for the maiden whom God had prepared for his master's son. In fact, he presented them to the virgin Rebecca as soon as he knew it was she.[262] There must be new garments for the Savior's spouse. If out of love for Him, she has stripped herself of her old affection for parents, country, home, and friends, she must now take on a completely new affection. She must love all these in due order, no longer according to human considerations, but because the heavenly Spouse wills, commands, and intends it so and has established such an order in charity.[263]

If we have once stripped off our old affection for spiritual consolation, devout exercises, practice of virtues, and even our own advancement in perfection, then we must put on another completely new affection, no longer loving all those graces and heavenly favors because they perfect and adorn our spirit, but because in them our Lord's name is sanctified in His kingdom, and His good pleasure glorified.

[261]Col. 3:9-10.
[262]Gen. 24:22, 53.
[263]Cf. Cant. 2:4 (RSV = Song of Sol. 2:4).

Finding God's Will for You

It is thus that St. Peter clothes himself in prison; not by his own decision, but in the way the angel commands him. He girds himself, next puts on his sandals, and then his other garments.[264] Stripped in a moment of all affections, the glorious St. Paul says, "Lord, what will You have me do?"[265] That is: "What do You want me to love, now that You have thrown me to the ground and have made my own will die within me?"

> Ah, Lord, put your good pleasure in its place,
> and teach me to do Your will, for You are
> my God.

Theotimus, the man who has forsaken all things for God must take back nothing except as God wills it. He does not nourish his body except as God ordains, so that it may serve the soul. He makes further studies only to serve his neighbor and his own soul in accordance with God's intention. He no longer practices virtues according to his own preferences, but according to God's desire.

God commanded the prophet Isaiah to strip himself completely naked. He did so, and went about and preached in this way for three whole days, as some say, or for three years, as others think.[266] Then, when the time set for him by God had passed, he put his clothes back on again.

We, too, must strip ourselves of all affections, both little and great, and make a frequent examination of our heart to see if it is truly ready to divest itself of all its garments, as Isaiah

[264]Acts 12:8.
[265]Cf. Acts 9:6.
[266]Isa. 20:2-3.

did. Then at the proper time, we must take up again the affections suitable to the service of charity, so that we may die naked upon the Cross with our divine Savior and afterward rise again with Him in the new man.[267] "Love is strong as death,"[268] to enable us to forsake all things. It is as magnificent as the Resurrection to adorn us with glory and honor.

---

[267]Rom. 6:4-6.
[268]Cant. 8:6 (RSV = Song of Sol. 8:6).

∞

Biographical note

St. Francis de Sales
(1567-1622)

Doctor of the Church and patron saint of writers, St. Francis de Sales was remarkable "not only for the sublime holiness of life which he achieved, but also for the wisdom with which he directed souls in the ways of sanctity."[269]

The eldest of thirteen children, Francis de Sales was born in 1567 to a noble family in the French-speaking Duchy of Savoy (an area straddling present-day eastern France and western Switzerland). He received a superb education in both France and Italy. Although intended by his father for a diplomatic career, St. Francis was ordained to the priesthood in the diocese of Geneva in 1593. Shortly thereafter, he was sent to the Chablais region of the Savoy on a mission to persuade those who had fallen under Calvinist influence to return to the practice of Catholicism. St. Francis spent four years laboring at this difficult task, during which he suffered many indignities. More than once he was thrown out of his lodgings, and had to sleep in the open air. Many times he celebrated Mass in empty churches or continued preaching while the congregation walked out. Nevertheless, St. Francis's unflagging poise and kindness in this mission led to its eventual success. By the turn of the

[269]Pope Pius XI, *Rerum omnium perturbationem*, 4.

century, the majority of the area's inhabitants had returned to the Catholic Faith.[270]

After his election as Bishop of Geneva in 1602, St. Francis continued his apostolic efforts to win souls back to the Catholic Church. At the same time, St. Francis sought to build a broad community of devout persons within the Church who would live the life of Christian perfection in all their varied states and vocations.[271]

It was St. Francis's absolute conviction that "holiness is perfectly possible in every state and condition of secular life," whether one is male or female, rich or poor, single or married.[272] He expounded this view at length in his classic work *Introduction to the Devout Life*. This conviction permeates the advice he gave to the many persons from all walks of life to whom he gave spiritual direction, both in person and in letters renowned for their spiritual wisdom, their psychological insight, their graciousness, and what one scholar has called their "inspired common sense."[273]

Jane Frances Frémyot, Baroness de Chantal, is the most famous of those who came to St. Francis for spiritual direction. An aristocratic young widow with four children, she met St. Francis in 1604. In cooperation with her, St. Francis founded the Visitation of Holy Mary in Annecy in Savoy, a congregation

[270]Ibid., 8.

[271]*Francis de Sales, Jane de Chantal: Letters of Spiritual Direction*, ed. Wendy M. Wright and Joseph F. Power (New York: Paulist Press, 1988), 23.

[272]Pius XI, *Rerum omnium perturbationem*, 13.

[273] Elisabeth Stopp, ed., *St. Francis de Sales: Selected Letters* (New York: Harper and Bros., 1960), 33-34.

for unmarried and widowed women who aspired to religious life but who were not sufficiently young, healthy, or free of family ties to enter one of the more austere women's orders of the day. The Visitation eventually developed into a cloistered religious order devoted to prayer and the cultivation of the "little virtues" St. Francis praised so highly. The order flourished during St. Francis's lifetime and afterward. St. Jane de Chantal was herself canonized in 1751.

After nearly thirty years of tireless labor on behalf of the Church and its members, St. Francis de Sales died of a cerebral hemorrhage in Lyons, France, on December 28, 1622. He had been traveling in the entourage of the king and queen of France at the time, but rather than stay in royal quarters, he lodged in the gardener's cottage on the grounds of the Visitation convent in that city. Fittingly for this apostle of the little virtues, he died in that modest cottage.

St. Francis de Sales was canonized in 1665. His feast day is celebrated on January 24.

∞

Sophia Institute Press®

An Invitation

Reader, the book that you hold in your hands was published by Sophia Institute Press.

Sophia Institute seeks to restore man's knowledge of eternal truth, including man's knowledge of his own nature, his relation to other persons, and his relation to God.

Our press fulfills this mission by offering translations, reprints, and new publications. We offer scholarly as well as popular publications; there are works of fiction along with books that draw from all the arts and sciences of our civilization. These books afford readers a rich source of the enduring wisdom of mankind.

Sophia Institute Press is the publishing arm of the Thomas More College of Liberal Arts and Holy Spirit College. Both colleges are dedicated to providing university-level education in the Western tradition under the guiding light of Catholic teaching.

If you know a young person who might be interested in the ideas found in this book, share it. If you know a young person seeking a college that takes seriously the adventure of learning and the quest for truth, bring our institutions to his attention.

www.SophiaInstitute.com
www.ThomasMoreCollege.edu
www.HolySpiritCollege.org

SOPHIA INSTITUTE PRESS

THE PUBLISHING DIVISION OF

Sophia Institute Press® is a registered trademark of Sophia Institute. Sophia Institute is a tax-exempt institution as defined by the Internal Revenue Code, Section 501(c)(3). Tax I.D. 22-2548708.